Poetry Now Young Wr… …rs

CO… …C!

SOUT… …PSHIRE

Edited by Carl Golder

First published in Great Britain in 1999 by
POETRY NOW YOUNG WRITERS
1-2 Wainman Road, Woodston,
Peterborough, PE2 7BU
Telephone (01733) 230748

HB ISBN 0 75430 297 0
SB ISBN 0 75430 298 9

FOREWORD

With over 63,000 entries for this year's Cosmic competition, it has proved to be our most demanding editing year to date.

We were, however, helped immensely by the fantastic standard of entries we received, and, on behalf of the Young Writers team, thank you.

The Cosmic series is a tremendous reflection on the writing abilities of 8-11 year old children, and the teachers who have encouraged them must take a great deal of credit.

We hope that you enjoy reading *Cosmic South Hampshire* and that you are impressed with the variety of poems and style with which they are written, giving an insight into the minds of young children and what they think about the world today.

CONTENTS

Louise Cobb	86
Scott Smith	86
David McAdam	86
Megan Butler	87
Emma Olliff	87
Aron Read	88
Lucy Hockham	88
Jonathan Daly	88
Jasmine Caminada	89
Joshua Bargh	89
Lucy Read	90
Zoe Crawford	90
Melanie Rocher	91
Ben Kett	91
Emma Joseph	92
Jennifer Keeping	92
Matthew Theobald	93
Amy Dyson	93
Calum Harris	94
Rebecca Woolgar	94
Sam Shepherd	95
Chloe Wallis	95
Katherine Fournier	96
Jon Clark	96
Michael Kealy	96

Orchard Junior School

Megan Baynham	97
Michael Naidoo	97
Daniel Humphries	98
Matthew Irwin	98
Ben McMonagle	99
Catherine Smith	99
Sarah Harding	100

THE POEMS

GRANDAD

Far away in a wonderland
There was a beach with red water and blue sand,
There was a candy store where everything was free
It had all the sweets from A to Zee,
It even had lollipops that looks like you and me,
Me with blonde hair and a bright blue dress,
And you in black, dressed in your Sunday best.
The mountains were ice-cream with cherries on top
When the train blew its whistle a big bubble popped.

The houses were made out of chocolate,
And chocolate sprinkles as soot.
We climbed up the ice-cream mountain and ate all day
Then went down and ate the blue sherbet on the bay
The moon was a cookie
And the stars spread crumbs in the sky.

Then we started swimming, swimming far away,
Suddenly we were home again under the cherry tree
Grandad and me!

Christanne Wicking (11)

NIGHT

When I go to bed at night I get a great big fright
When my mum turns off the landing light
I scream 'Mum I'm not asleep!'
Then Mum says 'Start counting sheep'
I get to a hundred and two then I need the loo.
I've been up here for nearly two hours
I wish I had some magic powers.

Romie Newman (10)
Brockenhurst CE Primary School

CAR JOURNEY

Face pressed against the window
Loads of bags in the boot
Brother on his Game Boy
Car behind swerves and hoots

Father swears
Brother stares
Swerving, darting, jolting
Now the journey's more exciting!

Red! Orange! Green!
We're out of the traffic jam at last
Driving alongside of the shops
Waving to everybody going past

Now the journey's getting boring
We're on the motorway again
Brother gets back to his Game Boy
It's a typical thing for him!

Only five minutes to go
It seems a really long wait
Turn the corner to granny's cottage
She's waving at the gate

The world's a big maze
When you're driving in the car
Especially when you're going on holiday
It's just too far!

Florence Kennard (10)
Brockenhurst CE Primary School

The Drive To The Match

Clive, Dad, me and Bea
Off to Barnet v Torquay
Jumped in the car

Then Bea said 'I want a choco bar'
Clive gave her one
And then said 'Golly this is really fun'
We all agreed and shouted *'Yeah'*

I was so excited, I was sure Barnet would win
Or I'd kick myself in the shin
Clive was a Torquay United fan,
Well, I always thought he was an odd man.

We travelled happily as if we knew the score
A total nil all draw!

Connie Karol Burks (9)
Brockenhurst CE Primary School

My Cat

My cat's very lazy,
She loves to sleep all day,
She goes out at night-time,
And comes in when it's day.

Food is all she's needing,
Nothing more than that
A warm place to sleep,
Stretched out on that mat,
I wonder why my cat
Doesn't get fat?

Peter Wooldridge (9)
Brockenhurst CE Primary School

Animal Bliss

Bees keep buzzing by my nose,
Birds keep singing a happy tune,
Butterflies hovering over a red, red rose.

Dogs in front of a fire,
Donkeys nibbling at a child's carrot,
Dromedaries sleeping in their byres.

Tree frogs cooling in leaf baths,
Turtles waddling up the beach,
Tigers waiting for antelopes to pass.

Elizabeth Kirk (10)
Brockenhurst CE Primary School

Mother's Day

Mother's Day that's today,
Which is why we'd like to say,
Mum we love you,
Mum we care,
Which is why we'd like to share,
All our love with you today,
That is what I have to say.

Huw Garrod (10)
Brockenhurst CE Primary School

Charlie's Haircut

Long, fluffy hair,
Dangling about,
He looks like a sheep,
He needs his hair cut.

Almost no hair at all,
Shivering and shaking,
Charlie has had his hair cut,
Wishing he hadn't had it cut at all.

Henry Streets (9)
Brockenhurst CE Primary School

WAITING

A child stands by a teacher,
This happens every day.
Standing silently by the teacher looking confused.
She is asking him a question, but he is quiet.
All around him there is a forest of hands,
Shouting 'Ask me! Ask me!'
The boy stands glum and embarrassed,
He scuttles back to his seat ashamed.
Another child gets the question right,
But she smiles kindly at him.

James Nurse (10)
Brockenhurst CE Primary School

I'M THINKING

I'm thinking of a poem,
But nothing comes to mind,
My mind is empty,
I cannot think,
My ideas are swirling down the sink
I think of St Lucia
And all the topics we've had
This is all I can think of, is it enough?

Katie Hunter (10)
Brockenhurst CE Primary School

Dream Island

Lazing dazing on
the sandy shore
not knowing what for
children playing
trees swaying
the sand is as
hot as the sun.

Coconuts, bananas
fruits galore
very friendly people
and much more.

Melting away
wanting to stay
time passing
o' so fast.
Time for tea
at last.

Hot and spicy chicken
and fish from the sea
this sunny island
is where I want to be.

Lucinda Hankin (9)
Brockenhurst CE Primary School

Droopy Jaws

I once knew a girl called Droopy Jaws
She had ears like taxi doors
But one thing that she always said was
Don't eat that fast
Make it last

Her teeth were white as white as could be
She liked to crunch ice cubes you see
Her hair was black as night
When I saw her I had a fright
I ran away as fast as I could
Down the lane and into the wood.

Mark Husband (9)
Brockenhurst CE Primary School

SAINT LUCIA

It is a small island
With lots of high mountains
Lots of sun
But it has great storms
Bananas here, bananas there, bananas everywhere
Sunny beaches
Hot sand
Yes you've named it *Saint Lucia!*

Nia Evans (9)
Brockenhurst CE Primary School

FLOWERS

Flowers, I like them because they are pretty.
Lovely flowers - watch them spring from the ground.
Opening flowers they look nice.
Wild flowers growing in the forest.
Elegant roses how beautiful they stand.
Racing flowers, I wonder which is going to be the tallest first.
Sometimes the sunflowers grow too tall for me.

Helen Baker (8)
Brockenhurst CE Primary School

The Forest

The leaves crunch beneath my feet,
As I walk slowly through the forest's trees,
The birds cheep merrily high in the sky,
The water falls into the rivers with an almighty crash.

Summer has come,
The trees have blossomed
The grass is rich and green
Children are playing happily everywhere.

Winter has struck and the cold has arrived,
The rivers are frozen and the air is cold,
No more children playing in the sun,
No more ice-creams in the park,
Snow and ice is all you get.

Jonathan Stratton (9)
Brockenhurst CE Primary School

Comics

Praise your comic,
love your comic,
read it at your will,
but when you buy it from the shop remember the bill!

Most comics make you laugh,
few are very sad,
though some comics you buy make you feel glad!

A comic tells us lots of things,
pollution in our world,
yes it tells us lots of things,
even how your mum's hair is curled!

Ben Money-Coomes (10)
Brockenhurst CE Primary School

SOAP

Slippy, slippy soap.
Jumps from my hand.
Slips into the tub,
With a splish, splash, splosh,
Where is it?
Where is it?
Mum took it out!
Oh! Oh! Oh!

Zara Cherry (9)
Brockenhurst CE Primary School

WALES

W ales is a great places to stay
A nd it's pretty crowded too.
L aughame is a place in the south of Wales.
E nglish and Welsh are spoken in Wales.
S wansea is a place in the south of Wales.

Jamie Lawrie (10)
Brockenhurst CE Primary School

A SMILE

Is worth nothing,
Until it has been given away,
For those who receive it,
Feel comfort and belonging,
And none need it so much,
As those who have forgotten
How to.

Lucy Wooldridge (11)
Brockenhurst CE Primary School

ALL ABOUT JEWELLERY

Silvery jewellery everywhere.
I wear it on my fingers
And I wear it in my hair.
I wear it on my ears
And I wear it on my toes,
If I'm going somewhere special
I sometimes pin it on my clothes.

I love earrings on my ears,
And colourful bracelets round my wrists.
Shiny rings on fingers,
Dangly necklaces round my neck.
Silver, emeralds, sapphires and rubies,
Gold, diamonds and pearls,
I love all kinds of jewellery from all over the world.

Elyse Paulson (5)
Brockenhurst CE Primary School

THE DENTIST

I'm always scared of visiting the dentist,
Waiting in terror for my name on the list.
The dentist says things like, 'Hello, how are you?'
To make you feel not so scared, but I still do.
As I lie there looking up his hairy nose
In the comfy chair I wouldn't mind a doze.
After a while he'll say all finished, all done,
I jump off the chair and put my coat back on.
Then the dentist has a quick chat with my mum
While I run down the street to get an iced bun.

Fiona Kelly (10)
Brockenhurst CE Primary School

Easter Eggs

Easter eggs
Yummy, yummy,
Chocolate eggs in my tummy.

Easter eggs
Chocolate bunnies
Lovely chocolate Easter eggs.

Chocolate Easter eggs
Chocolate Easter eggs
Chocolate Easter eggs.

Alice Rollin (10)
Brockenhurst CE Primary School

Car Journey

Seatbelts on, ready to go,
Clunk click the start of the trip,
Looking out the window lots of different views,
Seeing lots of people dodging the horse poos,
Lots of different cars all different shapes,
Ford, BMW and many other makes.
Round the corner and over the hill,
Hold on to your tummies or you'll be ill.
The journey is now coming to an end,
So we go up the road and round the bend.

Sara Hatton (10)
Brockenhurst CE Primary School

Sweets

Inside of the sweet packet,
There are sweets waiting to be eaten,
There are bars waiting to be munched,
And there are cough sweets waiting to be sucked.

Inside of the sweet packet,
There are rustling voices talking,
There are happy squeaks squeaking,
And there are fidgeting sweets moving.

Inside of the sweet packet,
There are glorious sweets in pink,
There are fantastic sweets in black,
And there are sunny sweets in yellow.

The sweet packet is slowly opening now,
And the sweets are no longer hiding,
One by one they are being eaten,
Until . . . there . . . are . . . none . . . left.

Sarah Covington (9)
Brockenhurst CE Primary School

Mother's Day

Mother's Day is when you give your mum
flowers and a card
You make the house lovely
and work very hard.

You make breakfast and a tray of tea
Make sure you're not busy, keep the day free.
We all love our mums, everyone has one
Mother's Day is special and jolly good fun.

Harriet Alcock (9)
Brockenhurst CE Primary School

GRAN'S HOUSE

Dropped off at Gran's house,
Knock on the door and go inside.
In the kitchen, looking through the window,
Seeing all the forest and the golf course.

As I go into the lounge I see loads of books
And games also a little Buddha statue.
In the lounge is an old record player and piano
Also a widescreen TV with Sky TV.

Out the French doors is the garden.
Down the garden steps is the forest
Where we make our bases.
Back in the house and up the stairs
Is my gran's bedroom and dressing room.
In the bedroom is a huge bed,
Under it is a huge spider with huge fangs, scary!

Down the landing is a spooky door,
And inside that room is another door
And in that are some scary steep steps
And down the bottom
I think wolves are going to run up to me, scary!

On the second floor are me and Hugh's bedrooms.
In Hugh's bedroom is a door to his balcony
And in my bedroom I have to climb out of the window!

On the three different balconies there is a Sky satellite.
I never go too near to the edge, I think I might fall off!

Anthony Greenwood (10)
Brockenhurst CE Primary School

TRAINS

Trains go fast
Some go slow
Trains go clonk
As they go
Clic clac goes a train
And they don't like the rain

Trains are noisy
They are loud
At a station
There is a crowd
The crowd is loud
Same as a train
And the crowd
Wait
For the train
In the rain.

James Hunter (7)
Brockenhurst CE Primary School

SPACE

Space is full of things to be found,
Like the stars all shiny and round.
No one knows how space came to be,
Space holds everything even you and me.
We send up ships to explore space,
To find creatures unknown to the human race.
Ugly things that are big and mean.
They are drawn in lots of colours mostly green.

Michael Baker (10)
Brockenhurst CE Primary School

PIANO EXAMS

Piano exams are nerve-racking,
Some of them are queer,
Sometimes they're quite scary,
I wish I had mine next year.

Some kids pretend to be ill on the day,
Weird infants think it's a bit of OK,
Some small wimps whine and say,
'I don't want to do my exam today.'

When you walk through the examiner's door,
You see him towering from the floor,
Then you take your place at the piano stool,
And hope that he doesn't think you're a fool.

My favourite piece is called 'Dew On The Grass',
If I do well I might get a present if I pass,
All in all pianos are OK,
But the problem is you have to practice every day.

Jason Noble (11)
Brockenhurst CE Primary School

SHEEP RAP

Of course, we are sheep,
But not the kind that help you sleep.
We don't follow you to school,
Because we are not that kind, you fool.
Baa baa black sheep, that's not true,
'Cause we are white, but not like you.
See we have wool to keep us warm.
Some to make a cardigan, some to make a hat,
And some to make a blanket, for your little cat.

John Hunter (10)
Brockenhurst CE Primary School

FUN

I like to ride bikes
Wild and peddling free,
Zooming up the garden
At top speed
Well - nearly.

I like to swing on the swing
And fly into the air,
Going to Jupiter, Saturn, Mars
Is Pluto there?

I like to swim and splash about
But don't say Mum I have to come out.
I am getting faster at my crawl
One day I know I'll beat them all.

Charlie Nurse (8)
Brockenhurst CE Primary School

POEMS

I hate writing poems,
That's probably why I'm no good,
I don't try 'cause it's boring,
But the teacher says I should,
So I sit down trying to write,
I ask the teacher what rhymes with sight?
I sit there sighing,
I must be lying,
I know how
To write poems,
Because - I'm writing one now.

William Rogers (11)
Curdridge Primary School

Summer

Summer comes but once a year,
And when it comes it brings good cheer,
The flowers bloom and the birds sing.

    The sun is hot,
    The water is cool,
    There is a dove flying above you.

Watch it turn watch it glide,
Through the sky,
The bird has stopped and so shall I.

    The summer is a special time of year,
    It's the time of year for picnics,
    And sing good cheer.

Charlie Smith (11)
Curdridge Primary School

The Birds' Song

In the field I wandered alone,
And high in the tree came a glorious tone
Of birds singing so sweetly their song,
As if in their life there was nothing wrong.
For some time I gazed with fascination,
Whilst the birds carried on with their conversation.
They built their nests of bits and bobs,
Every little bird had their own little jobs.
But the time had come for me to leave,
While they had fun, I alone in grief.

Kelly Jones (11)
Curdridge Primary School

TIGER

I am a tiger, the tiger of love
I am the king of the jungle
I rule the jungle, like a King
I am the prince of everything.
But you can say, I am the love
of the tiger.

But you could say I am the best
tiger in the world.
That is why the eyes of the tigers
are set on me.
My stripes are amber and black
and my crown is gold.
My teeth are sharp and my claws
are deadly.

James Barney (10)
Curdridge Primary School

SWIMMING

I put on my goggles
I put on my trunks
I wobbled to the end of the diving board
I jumped as high as I could
I landed in the pool
The lifeguard shouted tidal wave
But there was no water left in the pool
I realised everybody was wet
Oh dear!
Oh no!

Graham Marks (10)
Curdridge Primary School

EASTER

One night before going to bed,
I saw my mum and then I said
Have you seen the Easter bunny?
She said, 'No but he has a fat tummy.'

In the middle of the night,
I saw a very shining light!
Then I saw someone's shadow, not a bad habit,
Then the shadow came closer, it looked like a rabbit!

Then I saw the rabbit but it was not ordinary,
Because he looked very cartoony!
Then I realised he was really funny,
I turned on the light, it was Bugs Bunny!

I asked the question, 'Are you the Easter bunny?'
Bugs replied, 'Yes and I'm funny.'
In the morning when Bugs was gone,
Mum came in, something was wrong!

I was downstairs eating my breakfast,
For an Easter treat we went to Texas!
That's the end of Easter now.
I thought Bugs was well, *wow!*

Jackson Booth-Millard (10)
Curdridge Primary School

THE BMX RIDE

I was going down the half pipe on my BMX
When I suddenly saw a hovercraft coming into Portsmouth.
I slipped and flipped and was in a pile on the half pipe
With a buckled wheel and a bit of a muddle.

Mitchell Howepiper (10)
Curdridge Primary School

My Game

The ball was passed up on the wing
And then with a mighty swing
He passed it to me
And then passed it to mastermind Lee.

He dribbled it round the defender
And shot like a 'tremender'
He sent the goalie flying
Into the sun, where he came back down frying.

Out come the stretchers with the big red cross
You should have seen Lee, he thought he was the boss.
The coach subbed Lee
And luckily it was not me.

He threw Lee out the team,
His face was very mean.
It began to rain - it was very wet,
I kicked the ball in the back of the net.

The great roar broke out
And they all began to shout
Hooray for Petrovitch
Then I bent down and kissed the pitch.

By now the ground was soaking wet
The defender slipped into his own net
For then the striker gave a pound
And knocked the goalie to the ground.

Out come the stretchers, just one more
I got the ball just to score
This was strange the crowd did not roar
And that's because they'd all gone home!
Sorry but I've got to go
My mum is calling through the snow!

Peter Bush (10)
Curdridge Primary School

THE HUMMING FRIDGE

Humming away in the corner,
Keeping your food cool,
Silent till you open its door,
And then it goes into overdrive,
Trying to keep itself cold.

When it opens the light shines bright,
Lets you see the food within.
What would we do without it?
We would probably die,
Or our food might just go bad.

It's been brilliant all my life,
It could have saved it a few times,
I hope it will carry on saving lives,
Until I die and beyond,
Please let it continue or I'll cry.

It haunts the house at night-time,
Humming its joyful sound,
Hoping it will continue all my life
Helping me sleep,
For my midnight feast.

Benedict McNulty (10)
Curdridge Primary School

Spring

When spring comes it's a happy time,
When it comes you get a peace of mind.

You go outside in the fresh air,
In spring my favourite fruit is a pear.

Outside you see nice flowers,
You can just stay there for hours and hours.

On Good Friday Jesus died,
But luckily He rose and survived.

Soon into spring Easter comes,
Let's eat some chocolate *yum yum yum.*

Spring only comes once a year,
But when it does it's a good time to cheer!

Nick Giles (10)
Curdridge Primary School

Rosie And Squeak

Rosie and Squeak
Are two guinea pigs,
They aren't very small,
Yet they aren't very big.

Well they live in a hutch,
At the back of the house,
And they squeak,
And they scratch,
And it sounds like a mouse.

Amber Martin (10)
Curdridge Primary School

Nature

Ducklings in the big wide river,
Swimming from side to side,
Newborn lambs and baby calves,
Dancing around the field,
Ponies bucking and rearing around,
All the flowers are swaying,
Frogs are bouncing around the pond
Nature is so beautiful.

Rebecca Stephenson (9)
Curdridge Primary School

The Glittering Moon

I saw the moon up there
Bright and glittering.
He smiled down at me.
I smiled back at him.
Lovely moon, smiling moon,
Dancing moon.
Last night I saw my friend moon
Dancing up there, up there.

Miriam Goddard (10)
Curdridge Primary School

My Dog Sophie

My dog Sophie is brown and white
She sleeps in her box all through the night
She loves to play and loves to bark
But she loves me best of all!

Kirsty White (11)
Curdridge Primary School

Wondering

The butterflies are flying,
Flying in the wind,
And wondering why?

Why are they wondering?
Wondering why?
Nobody knows,
Only the wind knows, who blows them,
Blows them everywhere.

When night falls,
It covers the wind,
All is calm,
Calm like the sun,
In the beginning of summer,
In the beginning of summer,
Only the wind knows who blows them.

Isobel Cafe (9)
Curdridge Primary School

My Dream Butterfly

I had a dream about a butterfly.
She flew across the dazzling sky.
Her wings were made of silk and satin.
Her heart had a beautiful carved-out pattern.
She danced like the sun in the morning dew
Until she flew into a blending hue.
That was all I saw of that butterfly
But I remember her when I look into
The dazzling night's sky.

Sarah Foxon (10)
Curdridge Primary School

Daffodils

Those marvellous colours
Of orange and green,
That wonderful yellow
So bright, with such gleam.

They dance by the river
They sway by the lake,
What wondrous pictures
And memories they make.

While they lay in the meadow
With all their grace,
I seem to feel
A smile on my face.

And now they are going
With glorious cheer,
I whisper, just slightly,
I'll see you next year.

Kirsten Ferrari (11)
Curdridge Primary School

Eggs

Eggs are beautiful and curvy
Eggs are nice and round.
They come in different colours
But mostly come in brown.

Eggs are very special
They start a brand new life.
They are ever so exquisite
And also a delight.

Oliver Plaatsman (11)
Curdridge Primary School

THE SUMMER HOUSE

Among the Scottish hills and past the shallow lake,
The small summer house calls my name.
Memories come flooding back,
I remember my pleasant childhood and when I used to
Come here with my cousins.
We used to splash water out of the stone fountain.
I remember how nice and clean it tasted.
I remember the bird table,
Just outside the loving summer house.
The different birds sung and danced,
That filled the air with a safe feeling,
It was as if someone or something was holding me tight,
With strong arms.
I walk through the creaky doors of the summer house,
I feel young again.
But no one has been here for years,
No one visits my special place.
The summer house is no more.

Ruth Kemp (11)
Gomer Junior School

FRIENDS

Friends are there through all the day,
They make you laugh and make you cry,
They cheer you up when you are down,
They share your secrets you dare not tell.

Friends can either be big or small,
They can be in or out of school,
They may even be your next door neighbours,
My friends are there through the day.

Laura Lucking (10)
Gomer Junior School

Park Life

In the corner of the park,
Behind the light green nettles,
Under the great old oak,
Is where we always go.
Never are we disturbed,
We just watch the passing families.
Chatting about the things they see,
And all the gossip that's new.
There's Mr Jones the park keeper,
Reading his morning paper.
There's the local gang,
Big and bad with hair that looks
Like spines on a porcupine.
But don't worry they won't find us here.
There's the pub that sells the beer.
There's the bride here for her reception,
The guests, the bridesmaids,
The usher, the vicar. (What's he doing here?)
Now the sun streams through the thick oak branches.
I just lay back and relax.

Christopher Campbell (11)
Gomer Junior School

Cockles

Cockles, cockles, cockles galore
Cockles, cockles, on the floor
Cockles, cockles on the door
Cockles, cockles I want more.

Peter Loneragan (9)
Gomer Junior School

FRIENDSHIP

My best friend is kind,
how many times has he saved my behind?
I wish I had a million,
if not a trillion.
He has never frowned,
and he's never ever down.
He's not all that bad,
and never really mad.
Best friends are great,
but I really hate.
The arguments were in,
where he kicks me in the shin.
And hits me on the head,
so I have to go to bed.
And knee me in the back,
oh what a punch he packs.

Sam Beed (11)
Gomer Junior School

MY FRIEND SAM

My friend Sam is not quite tall,
Although you would not call him small.

His hair is orange like the sun,
He runs as fast as a bullet from a gun.

Basketball is his favourite sport,
All his skill I have taught.

He's always there when I am down,
I really like him being around.

Leon Chance (10)
Gomer Junior School

Uncle Chris

(In loving memory of Uncle Chris)

I see him now with his face bright pink,
He's on his dream bike,
Zooming down the road,
Without a care in the world.

He's got his dream.

He's in the lead,
With his friends up behind him.

He's got his dream

I see him now in his red and white tight-fitted
leather suit,

But now he's passed,
And now roaring his way,
Up to Heaven,
Nevertheless he will always be racing in my heart.

Emma Phillips (11)
Gomer Junior School

My Computer

My computer is full of fun with all its computer games.
My computer has Fury 3 with lots of different aims.

My computer is used for business and all my dad's accounts.
My mum adds up all the figures to get the final amounts.

My computer has a CD ROM for all my CD games.
We have Encarta and Monopoly and other well known names!

Shaun Reynolds (9)
Gomer Junior School

Space

In space you can't chase
You can't even do up your lace
That's what you can't do in space
In space you can see lots of stars
You see more and more
Especially on Mars
That's what you can see in space
In space the air is thin, thin as your hair
I wouldn't dare to breathe in the air
That's what the air is like in space
In space it's pitch-black
'Need a bright light' said Jack
That's how it is in space
In space when we go to a different planet
'How exciting' said Janet!
That's what we're like in space.

Chris Kingshott
Gomer Junior School

An Odd Man

I dreamed a dream while wide awake.
When I was walking on my hair and tongue.
I saw half man half woman on a chair
That wasn't even there.
Then an hour that took a minute.
I saw a ghost that I could not see.
Then I fell on the floor when I was standing up.
When I walked to my mum when going to the pet shop
Then a dog that I saw who was a centimetre big ate me up.

Jake Light (9)
Gomer Junior School

BULLIES!

Nothing beats the loneliness
Nothing beats the pain
Nothing beats the humiliation
When they try again.

Nothing beats the feeling
That they're never going to stop,
Nothing stops the thinking
That they're going to come top.

You don't know how it feels
Until you've been through it
The bullies, stupid people
Feel they have to do it.

They kick you, punch you, hurt you, taunt you.
The feeling for the rest of your life will haunt you.

That's what bullies can do to you,
But don't let it show, that's what they want you to do!

Ian Watkins (10)
Gomer Junior School

HOW TO MAKE A RATTLESNAKE

Head like a round ball,
Eyes dark green, so that it can't be seen,
Tongue like bubblegum,
Fangs red with blood,
Tail like a maraca going thud thud thud.

Shirilee Shearman (8)
Gomer Junior School

My Pet Fish

My pet fish likes to wish
That's my pet fish

My pet fish
Swims around in a dish
He is very small
He has a little wall

My pet fish likes to wish
That's my pet fish

My pet fish is very fast
I say goodnight to him last
He likes to feed
In his dish there is some weed

My pet fish likes to wish
That's my pet fish

He has a nice wash
He's got lots of dosh
He has a nice rock
He likes to swim in Portsmouth dock

My pet fish likes to wish
That's my pet fish

Hayley Burns (9)
Gomer Junior School

Dad

I love my dad, he's very tall
but me and my sister are very small.
When we go to play football
he is the best of all.
I love my dad, he's very tall
but me and sister are very small.

I love my dad, he's very tall
but me and my sister are very small.
My dad is very mad
but he is glad of me and my sister.
I love my dad, he's very tall
but me and my sister are very small.

Anthony Lowman (9)
Gomer Junior School

NAN

My nan - she was the best
Always kind - but she did detest
People calling round when she was eating
She said one day she'd give 'em a beating!

Nan was generous - Nan was caring
She always looked cool - whatever she was wearing.
She always gave us sweets and other delicious little treats.
Like swiss rolls, jam tarts, hula hoops tons of ice-cream
in these big bowls (yum!).

In the autumn if we begged her please!
She would let us have apples off her apple trees.
In the winter we'd have apple pie, hot chocolate and go to the
park (that was great!)

In the boiling summer we'd play in her garden - swimming in the luke-warm water, football, and making things while Nan sat and watched.

In the spring we'd watch the infuriated bees.
I wouldn't have swapped my nan for anything!
R I P. . .

Claire Kimber (10)
Gomer Junior School

My Place On The Stairs

I have a place on the stairs,
Where I sit and wonder about the things
I would like to know.
Why do stars shine so brightly at night?
Why does a cat's tail curl like a question mark?
Why do birds sing so sweetly in the morning?
And why does sleep seem so short,
Yet it is so long?

My place on the stairs is special to me,
Because I can go there any time,
And tell it all my troubles,
It will never answer back.
It will always be there for me.
It will always be special.

Catherine Speed (11)
Gomer Junior School

The Kitchen

Beans beans yummy beans all over my jeans.
Grated cheese on my knees.
Coke Coke all over my cloak.
Melted Mars bar what a palaver.
Apple juice in a chocolate mousse.
I thought, I thought I'll have some more.
I got some crisps and gave 'em to Chris.
I want more, I want more, I want more.
Runny custard in the mustard.
Orange squash in the wash.
I brought a leek in the week.
I just want more.

Sam Webber (10)
Gomer Junior School

My Sister Saskia

I wake up in the morning,
Listening to tears,
She's crying.

I ask her what's the matter,
She does not answer,
I get worried.

I try and make her happy,
But the tears still come,
Why won't she stop?

It's time for school,
Please stop,
You're making me sad.

I finally get to her,
She tells me what's wrong,
It's her feet.

I rub and rub,
But nothing works,
I wish she was better.

I go to school feeling down,
I worry a lot,
I can't stop thinking about her.

I finish school.
It's all over,
I storm home like Concorde.

'She's fine' Mum says,
What a relief,
I'm glad she's alright.

Kurt Sheehan (11)
Gomer Junior School

RIVER HAMBLE

Boats row upstream,
Slowly, slowly.
Ripples go round in a golden glow
Round, round.
The river's sound echoes for miles,
Filling the forest with new life.
The gentle waves shine and gleam,
While they lap quietly on the shore.
I climb up the soggy bank and sit down,
I look out at the sparkling lake.
I feel like I've walked down memory lane,
Remembering all the things
I have done here.
My place is quiet and run down,
But I will always like my special place,
Whatever happens.

Natasha Ellwood (10)
Gomer Junior School

MY BEST FRIEND

My best friend is always there,
To tell me jokes, to laugh and share.
She's the one to be there each day.
She's reliable, friendly, never shy.
You might think it's all a lie,
She will be the one to make my day.
Every day and every night I make a wish
That one day we will be alike.
She is my best friend - I tell her all my secrets.
I never ever tell her a lie
It's the look in her soft brown eyes!

Hayley Breeze (10)
Gomer Junior School

My Grandad

My grandad is really kind,
  You'll never know what you'll find.
He'll always play a game,
  he'll never forget my name!
What a wonderful man he is.

My grandma says we're like two little kids,
  My grandad says I'm on the skids.
I think that means I'm going to lose,
  But I rarely do when I get to choose.
What a wonderful man he is.

Sometimes I go to the shops for him,
  I must admit he's not that slim!
He really does spoil me,
  We sometimes have a cup of tea.
What a wonderful man he is.

Georgina Sculthorpe (11)
Gomer Junior School

Giggs Got The Ball

Giggs got the ball on the centre line
A tap to the left - he's past Bostick.
A whack to the right - he's nearly lost it!
Is he going to try to shoot?
Oh yes, what a boot!
The goalkeeper's under par
Oh no! It's hit the bar!
He kicks the rebound - it's in the net!
That's one shot - he won't regret. . .

Rory Coughlin (9)
Gomer Junior School

My Topsy Turvey Poem

I was alive when I was dead!
I stuck a pencil in my head!
A ning nang nong came along
And sang me a rock and roll song!

I was flying in the sky - while sitting on the ground!
A no legged dog walked towards me!
And his stomach was very round!

It was light when it was dark!
He went to school when at the park!
The trees were dull and very light!
The mud was smooth but full of lumps!

Steven Raistrick (9)
Gomer Junior School

One Small Corner Of A Never-Ending Space

I put it in blackness,
A space so small no one can fit in,
It's gone now,
No one can find it,
They will never find it,
For only I know where it is.

A small corner of a never-ending space,
I put it there,
A place no one has been,
It is lost in dark, inky black,
A place that's not on any map,
Just put at the back of a shadow.

Gwyn Rees (11)
Gomer Junior School

THE MAGIC BOX

I will put in my box
The dragon from the Welsh flag
That is red and vicious,
All the books I have read in the long past,
The moon and the planets that are up in space.

I will put in my box
The North and South Poles that glimmer,
The seas that swish around night and day,
My whole family that I love so dearly.

My box is fashioned with the
Glimmer of a shining star,
The goldest gold,
And the changing skin of a chameleon.

I will swim in my box in the biggest ocean
And land on the biggest island.

Simon Richards (10)
Gomer Junior School

CHOCOLATE MONSTER LAND

A land where chocolate monsters live.
Chocolate monsters are nice to eat.
Everything I can see is made of chocolate - except for me!
I feel safe - no one can eat me!
All day I eat chocolate.
All night I eat chocolate.
I lie in a field feeling sick.
I begin to turn into chocolate myself.
I get so fat that I explode.
Chocolate everywhere!

Andy Smith (7)
Gomer Junior School

My Sister's Stir Fry

Not a lot of chicken
But an awful lot of rice.
Not a lot of cockroaches
But an awful lot of lice!
So if you want a tasty snack
Then now's the time to go and pack
You never know!
You might want to eat it in your house!

Thomas Patience (9)
Gomer Junior School

Circus Clown

There once was a circus clown,
Known as Billy Boy frown
He was in such a hurry
He fell in a curry
And came out covered in brown!

Kirsty Atkins (9)
Gomer Junior School

My Topsy Turvey Poem

The sun was out - in the middle of the night!
I was in bed asleep - flying my kite
After I flew my kite -
I woke to fall asleep!
I heard a bird sing - but without a beak!

John Mackay (8)
Gomer Junior School

SCHOOL

Wake up late!
School's started!
Detention at first break.
Julie's got my pencil case,
'Miss, Miss! I forgot my PE kit,
Do I really have to do it in my underwear?'
English now - spelling test,
'Lost my test book Miss!'
It's playtime - out to play except Joan.
Detention now
End of break, everyone in,
Maths test - no talking - what is 305 + 621?
'Tom dear, do you know?'
'Is it 926?'
'Well done!'
I can't find my pencil,
Lunch-time, out to play,
What's for dinner today?
End of break,
Silent reading,
Shh Joan!
Art now, paint a picture of a flower.
Pack up - home time!
'What's for tea Mum?'
'Fish and chips dear.'
Hurry up!
Go on! Bedtime oh!
Yes! Parents' evening tomorrow!

Harriet Roser (10)
Gomer Junior School

My Favourite Sport Is Football

My favourite sport is football.
It makes my mum so mad,
At half-past eight she says 'It's late'
And so I ask my dad!

'Oh Dad, oh Dad - come on be fair!
You know I'm nearly nine -
Let me watch the second half
I'm sure it will be fine!'

'Go on Dad - be on my side.
It's better when you ask her,
And if I'm late just one more time
It won't be a disaster!'

Thomas Wilkinson (8)
Gomer Junior School

Winter Wonders

Winter wonders, they all creep
In the night, when you're asleep!
Leaves frost on the winter ground.
There's always a white line of snow around.
Freezes lakes, ponds and rivers.
Gives all animals cold shivers.
But in the spring, the cold will go
And the sun will soon thaw the thick blanket of snow.
The sun will come out
And the summer flowers will sprout
From the sky - warm showers of rain
And nature's year - starts all over again!

Nicole Way (9)
Gomer Junior School

I'M MAD!

In the next millennium
In the year 2003 the taxis will be black cabs.
But that is in *um*
Oh 5 years and I will be 15.
I can not do this poem it will take me a day or even two.
My brain is going mad and this poem is so hard.
I don't want to do this any more.
I've got to say bye bye.
Au revoir, au revoir, au revoir!

Russell Todd (9)
Gomer Junior School

THE LADY FROM BATH

There was a young lady from Bath
Who tripped on a very bumpy path.
She fell onto a stone
And broke a bone
And everyone started to laugh!

Eleanor Cass (8)
Gomer Junior School

SCRAPYARD

Cinquain

Scrapyard!
Cars all smashed up
Cars piled high to the sky
I feel sad they are all smashed up.
Scrapyard!

Simon Metcalf (10)
Gomer Junior School

Under The Coffee Table

Under the coffee table.
The place where I go.
When upset or feeling mad
Under I go!

When I'm there I can't see much
Not at all!
As dark as the night-time sky.

Looking up,
Thinking about - not a lot!
Not at all!
Your mind is blank!

Everything's strange -
But it is still my special place!

Alex Murton (10)
Gomer Junior School

Raindrops

R ain makes the grass damp
A raindrop is running down the window sill
I t runs as fast as it can
N ever ever stops running down
D rip, drip, drip - always dripping
R ain makes the flowers grow
O n the grass you can see little dewdrops
P retty little flowers with rain to help them grow
S plash, splash - I splash in the puddles.

Jacqueline Malcolmson (8)
Gomer Junior School

Beth

(My Dog)

Anger, let down, hurt and sadness.
All put in one when she died
She was special to me.
She ran, she cried, she died,
Why did she die!
That is a question no one knows or will ever know.
Under the moon and far away.
I wait patiently to see the face of her again.
Her name was Beth
She was special to me.
I miss her!

Luke Phillips (11)
Gomer Junior School

My Grandma

(Renga)

Grandma loves baking
She likes baking scones and buns.
I love my grandma!

She has peach soft skin
Eyes like jewels that always shine
Hair that is shiny grey.

Alfie barks like mad
Early bed my grandma said
Grandma loves baking!

Joanne Tinling (11)
Gomer Junior School

The Field

I like the field
With tall trees to climb and swing
A sandpit to dig
A river to the seaside
And my den's in the bushes!

Ian Harvey (11)
Gomer Junior School

The Rain

The rain is the waterfall
The rain is the sea
The rain is all different
Things that I can see.
The waterfall is lovely
The waterfall is bright
It's such a good sight!

Suzanne Chance (8)
Gomer Junior School

Grandmas

(Tanka)

Grandmas are anxious
Nervous at letting you out.
In case you get hurt.
Got the time to talk to you
Because parents go to work.

Carl Regan (10)
Gomer Junior School

The Glitter Fairy Dance

I'd love to go to the place
Where the fairies dance
The fairies glance
The fairies sing
The fairies have a rainbow song
The fairies have a poem to sing
All the glitter fairies are my favourite friends
The fairies have a lovely voice
The fairies are a wonderful couple
The fairies have a wonderful band
It sounds like the summer and the spring
It is wonderful!

Danielle Wade (7)
Gomer Junior School

My Brother

(Renga)

Golden hedgehog hair
Gleaming, shining, deep blue eyes
Loves his toy - *Gromit!*

Working hard at school
Tongue out for concentration
Loves his toy - *Gromit!*

Imaginative
Creative, good at drawing
Terror of the house!

Jessica Lafferty (10)
Gomer Junior School

THE FOREST

Night has come to dwell upon the forest.
The sky looks like raging waters above the trees.
I fall asleep upon the grass.
Rainfalls with streets of thunder.
A tree cracks.
I look around the pitch-black woods.
The grass moves, the trees crack and creak.
I fall asleep - the rain dies down, the forest is calm.
The sun is up - I move and walk across the dewdrop grass.

Matthew Sellstrom (10)
Gomer Junior School

MY FAVOURITE PLACE

Somewhere where the sunshine glitters
And the rainbow spills its sparkling colours and drifts away.
Unicorns tip their falling powers
Into the magical wind that takes it where the meadows are gold
And shining colours pop out of the glowery grass.
It smells like honey taking the anger away
And in the distance looking like daffodils.
The moon comes out and at night dreams take over your head
And send you into a soundless sleep!

Joseph Nelson (8)
Gomer Junior School

BEHIND THE DOOR

Behind the door, with the brass knob,
I sit alone with all my thoughts,
With all my favourite books and toys,
A diary with a rusty key,
A fluffy pink bunny with a missing eye.

Behind the door, with the brass knob,
Away from the arguing, the shouting, the teasing,
Piles of books and toys surround me,
I sit alone with all my thoughts!

Lauren Murton (10)
Gomer Junior School

Raindrops

R ain sounds like pitter, patter, pitter
A nd thunder sounds like a bang!
I think lightning is colourful
N othing but raindrops everywhere!
D own the streets - here and there
R oar goes the thunder like flashing lions
P ure thunder, pure lightning - I don't know
O ut goes the gleaming snow
S now is gleaming white!

Michael Austin (7)
Gomer Junior School

Rainbow Poem

Red is an apple, as juicy as can be.
Orange is a fruit, its skin is as rough as the sea.
Yellow is the sun, that shines upon me.
Green is the grass and is long and tall.
Blue is the sky, which holds up the clouds.
Indigo is the night-time sky, with the stars twinkling down on me.
Violet is a flower and it grows so beautifully!

Emily Webb (8)
Gomer Junior School

Grandad

Every time I close my eyes,
I think and then I see my special person
In my mind
Hopefully thinking of me!

He had a wrinkly forehead
A friendly welcoming face
I think of him all the time
Although he's in that cloudy place!

He wore a checked hat and shortened trousers
He had a long brown pipe and a short grey jumper.

I hadn't seen him for much of my life
Just 'til I was seven
I see him in my mind now
Because he's in the place I like to call heaven!

Gillian Cooper (11)
Gomer Junior School

My Grandad

(Renga)

I love my grandad
He always gives me big hugs
His eyes are like diamonds.

We sit and tell jokes
On his furniture of oak
Laughing all around.

Play games all the time
His walls are painted with lime
I love my grandad!

Amy Duncan (10)
Gomer Junior School

Out Of This World

One day I met an alien
The alien was green.
I smiled at the alien,
And asked him where he'd been!

The alien answered slowly,
In a burbly sort of way
'I've been on a trip of a lifetime
It was a package holiday!'

'We went round the cosmos
In a cosmic plane.
We saw the sun, the moon, the lot
And off to Earth we came!'

'Pluto, Neptune, Uranus, Saturn,
Jupiter, Mercury, Venus, Mars
To all of them we've been
But why do you think we like your Earth?
Because your Earth's so green!

Oliver Cutting (9)
Horndean Junior School

Cosmic

Far away on a cosmic planet
In a cosmic universe
Where there's rockets booming
And stars shining
There's a little alien all alone
Who's bored and lonely,
But then along came an astronaut one day
And they became cosmic friends!

Paul Greig (9)
Horndean Junior School

Cosmic Beings

There's a cosmic world in outer space
Where every cosmic being has a wonky face.
Their eyes are in the middle, their mouths are at the top,
Their noses are at the bottom, if you saw one, you'd laugh till you drop.
But you won't catch me laughing - oh no! Not me!
Because to those cosmic beings on their cosmic world,
Maybe our faces just look like another lump of mould.
To me those cosmic beings really are a mystery,
So I would like to visit them, not you - me!
Those cosmic beings also have green and blue hair.
If you saw one - wouldn't you stare!
But you wouldn't be the only one to stare at someone new,
'Cos those little cosmic beings would be staring straight at you!

Catherine Sandwell (10)
Horndean Junior School

Phrases From Pluto!

(This Classroom's Such A Mess)

What on Pluto's going on!
What a *leffuh-leffub!*

There's paper all over the ceiling
And paint all over the floor!
Plus the wall carpet's dirty!
Mind you! Didn't you even bother to put the paint brushes
back in the fruit bowl?
The marbles aren't in the paint box!
And the fruit's on the classroom display,
Not in the marble sack!

Rachel Ballam (9)
Horndean Junior School

COSMIC

Can you hear the rockets roar and rumble?
Over the skies see stars tumble?
Saturn, Venus, Jupiter and Mars,
Mingling in-between the stars.
I wish I could travel up into space.
Climb up and find my own special place!

Matthew Carter (10)
Horndean Junior School

WHALE SONG

Blue and graceful
Splashing up to me
Floats as graceful and harmless as a whale
His song is like a bird in a tree.

As his fins splash he sings
His face is beautiful
His tail splashing at me
A hidden smile you can't see
Hides a secret from you and me.

The whale is as happy, as happy can be
But it swims right up to me one day in alarm
'Whale catchers have come to catch you!'
I say 'Do not kill him, he is my only friend!'

Whale, I do love you so
I never want to let you go
Here comes a wave to take you home
I will see you tomorrow, whale.

Elizabeth Todd (8)
Hulbert Junior School

THE SOLAR SYSTEM

In history six planets, now nine planets.
Comets flying here and there.
Satellites circle Earth,
Aliens! No aliens.
Galaxies going on - on like a bottomless pit.
Many rhymes fit the planets.
Spaceship ends floating.
Mercury the hot
Venus the great
Earth the living
Mars the red
Saturn the lazy
Uranus the chatterbox
Neptune the ill
Pluto the same
Red, blue, yellow - stars always exploding.
Earth - only one with life and water.
Mars maybe has life - or no life.
Does Pluto have life?
Mysteries to solve,
Do any planets have life?
That is the question;
But what is the answer!

Philip Salmon (10)
Kings Copse County Primary School

Cosmic

Aliens living in outer space,
Don't know much about the human race,
They board their rockets at ten to nine,
A clumsy alien broke his spine,
Their leader's name was Cosmic Sven,
They reached planet Earth at five to ten,
Their leader said 'Let's find their queen,
I'm sure she's not going to be green,'
They went to the queen and their leader said,
'Have you got a sofa or a comfy bed?'
The queen was shocked with what she saw,
There were fifty thousand aliens at her door,
She wouldn't let them in but they did not care,
They just let out their pet which was a grizzly bear,
The queen changed her mind and said 'Oh do come in'
They danced around the living room and made a din,
The queen soon had a plan which was quite supreme,
She gave them all some chocolate and some nice ice-cream,
The aliens fell asleep and the queen was quite content,
When she wrapped them in a plastic coated big round tent,
Then threw them on their rocket and they all went back to space,
They still don't know that much about the human race!

Jack Owen (11)
Kings Copse County Primary School

In Space

Are there aliens in space?
Do aliens have legs?
Do they have four eyes?
Is one eye on an antennae?
Do they have rough skin?
With lumps and bumps!

Do aliens live on far away planets?
Are the planets big?
Or are they small?
Are they really colourful?
Or are they really dull?
Do they have rings around them?
Or do they just float around!
Alone in the role of darkness!

Do aliens travel in spaceships?
Do the spaceships have shining armour?
Red, blue, green, orange and yellow maybe!
Do they have bomb blowers at the back
To blow up the enemy!
Is there a large periscope peeping
Out of the top to look around!

What do aliens have for entertainment?
Do they look at the stars?
Do they have quizzes naming the
Pictures of the stars?
Do aliens gather together in crowds
To see a shooting star?
I wonder . . .

Georgia Swain (10)
Kings Copse County Primary School

Cosmic

I have been a cosmic puppy,
I don't see him very much.
He plays with astronauts,
And other things as such.

He's been on many holidays,
To Jupiter and Mars.
He always gets the autograph,
From all the famous stars!

I once taught him to do a trick,
And offered him a treat.
Now give him a Milky Way or Mars,
And he'll stand up on two feet.

We went to Planet Hollywood,
And Arnie came to stay.
He said to Cosmic 'I'll be back!'
And then marched on his way.

By the way I named him Pluto,
I really can't think why.
But that would be another poem,
So until then, goodbye!

Louise Coggins (11)
Kings Copse County Primary School

Once When I Was Walking

Once I met a cosmic man
out walking with his cosmic dog
named Milky Way
shame about the name
named after a chocolate bar
what is the world coming to?
Then I saw an ad in the Daily Planet
is someone selling chicken legs
or just chipolatas?
Then I saw a sign
'The end of the Earth'
Whoopee!
At last I'll meet my match again
but not in the same dream
please.

Joe Thornewill (10)
Kings Copse County Primary School

Cosmic

I'm riding on my motor bike,
All the way through space,
I've just stopped at Jupiter,
I'm picking up a pace.

I see some cosmic monsters,
Going munch, munch, munch,
I zoom away so quickly,
Just in case I am their lunch!

I look ahead, I see a plough,
And it is made of stars,
If you look behind you'll see,
The planet they call Mars.

This is all you'll hear from me,
I can't go on all night,
I've got to go to Pluto now,
I'll soon be out of sight!

Lucy Mellors (11)
Kings Copse County Primary School

Cosmic

I'm riding in my spaceship
As rusty as it can be.
I'm feeling rather peckish
I might just have some cheese.
I'm looking round and round
To see what I can find.
There in front of me I see
An alien's behind!
The alien turns to see me
I jump out of my skin
'My name is Captain Cosmic
I'm always in a spin.'
He opened up his rucksack
And in it was some food
He shouted 'Moonsdale anyone?'
And in a flash he'd gone!

Christine Morgan (11)
Kings Copse County Primary School

THE KING OF THE SKY

If I was the king of the sky, the cosmos would be my kingdom.
The stars, the moons, the planets would be within my power.
The stars would be the jewels shining like a crown,
The clouds a fluffy throne for me when I sit down.
The moon would be my night light.
The planets would be my toys with great big open spaces
for me to dance with joy.
The sun would warm the rain for me to shower at night.
With all these things around me I think I'll be alright!

Lauren Brenton (10)
Kings Copse County Primary School

A COSMIC PLACE

There's a place I go to every day,
It's really cosmic, just like space.
There's a place to play,
A place to eat,
A place to do whatever you wish.
So come on down to this cosmic place
You never know,
This cosmic place might be in space.

Nicholas Ellis (11)
Kings Copse County Primary School

What I Think

When I look at the stars,
My thoughts stray to what they are,
Maybe they're fireflies or diamonds,
Or angels with no cover from the clouds,
Or the planets so round like a ball,
Like marbles in a bag.
Though scientists proved they are chunks of rock
And balls of gas, my mind will never know.

Sam Glaves (11)
Kings Copse County Primary School

Cosmic

C osmic is like floating in space.
O bjects flying in space and walking on the moon.
S hooting stars coming from the sky.
M any people walking on the moon.
I deas shooting around in space.
C osmic is calm and still in space.

Garrie Silverthorn (9)
Kings Copse County Primary School

Cosmic

C osmic is a place in space,
O n the moon you can see its face.
S ee the wonderful stars at night,
M ake the sky light up bright.
I nto space I will go,
C ome and see the world I know.

Katherine Churcher (9)
Kings Copse County Primary School

Cosmic

C osmic, like a ball of fire flying in space.
O ver in space aliens fly around like bumper cars.
S hooting stars fill the air with lovely colour.
M any people watch the sky to wonder what is going on up there.
I see lots of strange objects out in space.
C osmic, like the biggest star of all, the moon.

Thomas Brown (10)
Kings Copse County Primary School

The Force Of The Ocean

From the rock you could see the dark grey banks of cloud racing in
over the thrashing white horses moving in remorselessly to the coast.
The crashing sea was rapidly turning grey and angry.
It feverishly crashed into the soaked rocks of the beach.
The incoming tide driving in and sucked back out.
The sea was going through a grim metamorphosis.

You could feel the fury as the heaving ocean hit the rough,
jagged cliff side.
It was like a blackish monster trying to smash the rocks with every
pounding wave.
A wave hit the cliff and it crumbled under the pressure but these were
just storm waves the rest to come were much worse.
A gush of green water pounded at a rock causing it to break away.

A few hours passed, the sea was calm and the beach was nothing but
seaweed and soggy sand and as for the rocks they were carried away
by the force of the ocean.

Paul Murphy (11)
Locks Heath Junior School

The Raging Sea

The sea was crying with envy,
then falling limply off the rocks into the tiny pools
which once used to be full of life.

By now the white horses were gathering out at sea,
waiting to come in full impact against the cliff face.

Now the sea had turned into a writhing grey beast
who was spitting its fury on the rocks,
like a very angry one-humped camel.

The sea robbed the sand of its precious shells as it
thundered towards the cliff face with all the momentum
and violence of the deep, angry ocean.

Mark Clague (10)
Locks Heath Junior School

Free Like The Sea

I turned and coming towards me was he,
He who ebbed up like a writhing grey monster
Lashing upon the cliffs.
Upturning and shattering the helpless creatures
Struggling . . . squirming - never free.
He then pulled back to gather up strength
For another great attack.
Again and again he would whip, crash, tumble,
Pound and smash endlessly.
I did not feel fear, I felt something else.
Maybe it was interest, curiosity, excitement
Or just being free . . .
. . . free, free like the sea.

Vivien Ingrams (10)
Locks Heath Junior School

Everyday Sea Moods

The sea was calm,
Peaceful,
Running over the soft sand and smooth stones
With a whisper of gentleness.
The tide ran up the shore,
Repeatedly,
Like a child breathing in its sleep.

Gradually,
The sky darkened,
With the threat of thunder, lightning and strong winds.
Within a few seconds
It had whipped up the waves of the sea,
Which
Was now surging with rage,
All the momentum and violence of the ocean.
Enough to discard the whisper of gentleness.

It hurled itself against the rocks,
Like a gasping monster strangling its prey.

Then the wind died down,
Slowly but surely the sea was calm once more.

Matthew Quinn (11)
Locks Heath Junior School

The Story Of The Sea

The sea was white with excitement.
It moved remorselessly to cover the rocks.
It covered big and small,
and tall and thin,
as the sea came in,
like the dark grey enormous clouds,
rolling in from the Pacific.
Then the sea drew back
as if someone had pulled the plug,
but swiftly returned with a renewed force
like white horses charging at their enemies.

The ships were tossed and turned like toy boats in a rippled pool.
My torch shone brightly
on the dark black sea,
then the sea calmed down.
I heaved a sigh of relief,
as I settled on the sand
and the cold water lapped under my feet.
I shivered,
as I felt the cold of the white night
then fell asleep, by the green murky sea.

Stephanie Castell (10)
Locks Heath Junior School

The Mighty Deep

Behold the wonders of the mighty deep,
Where crabs and lobsters learn to creep.
Fish and sea horses learn to swim,
And clumsy sailors tumble in!

Behold the wonders of the mighty deep,
Where lucky divers get a magical peep.
And if you're swimming you sometimes find,
What sailors from the past have left behind.

Behold the wonders of the mighty deep,
Where fish and sea creatures always sleep.
Where waves are crashing,
And water is splashing.
Behold the wonders of the mighty deep.

Sarah Fletcher (10)
Locks Heath Junior School

The Cruel Powerful Sea

The sea reared its angry white head,
It moved remorselessly towards the girl who was all alone,
The incoming tide thrashed like a lion in distress against the cliff,
The calm ocean was now not only ugly, but deadly,
The devil pulverised the rock with each crushing wave,
As she climbed, the sea died weakly on the rock around her,
Mighty squally waves sneaking in,
Full of the devastating force of the deep ocean,
Cherry slid into the churning, frothing rock pools,
She climbed high but a huge green tower of water
cast her back on the rocks below,
Drowning, sinking under the green blanket of the sea.

Jason Clarke (10)
Locks Heath Junior School

The Battle

The waves were swirling, twisting round
Like an eel out of control.
They were smashing against the rock face
As if they were thunderbolts falling from the sky,
War-like, powerful weapons.

The dark grey rolling waves were crashing
Into the sharp, jagged cliffs,
Like a battleship being wrecked.

I felt alone, cut off, dumbstruck.
Would I survive against this fierce, violent enemy?

Michael Cutting (10)
Locks Heath Junior School

The Sea

The sea is like a whale,
Destroying ships and squirting water.

The sea is like a watering can,
Spreading water here and there.

The sea is like some Scottish raiders,
Attacking the cliff and taking the sand.

The sea is like a large container,
Keeping the ships and hiding the weed.

The sea was like an abandoned bath,
Sitting lonely with nothing but water.

Paul Venn (9)
Locks Heath Junior School

A Walk Down The Shore

I can taste the salty
sea water in my mouth.
And the fierce cold winds
blowing through my hair.

Bright white dead cuttlefish
lying like slippers on the shore.
Gulls crying and flying overhead.

Slimy seaweed running like wet paint
and pebbles crunching beneath my feet.

Shells of different shapes and sizes,
pebbles shining like diamonds on the golden sand.

Waves are like white horses racing against each other,
sand catching pools of rippling water.

Crabs are burying deep beneath the sand
and I gather up my memories into my mind.

Sophie Webb (9)
Locks Heath Junior School

City In Darkness

The lights twinkled,
Then darkness was sprinkled amongst the skyscrapers.
The blackout was like a disease spread over New York.
The blackout towered higher than high.
Over the skyscrapers.
Women were screaming,
And the cats stopped their preening and watched.

Laura Turner (9)
Locks Heath Junior School

THE GIANT'S NECKLACE

She was so busy collecting shells,
The dark clouds she did not see,
They were rolling in from the Atlantic,
And gathering menacingly.
They hid the face of the soothing sun,
And the evening grew quite cold,
But thirty shells she must collect,
And perhaps she was too bold.

White horses galloped towards the girl,
As she knelt on the sandy shore,
Then she heard the wailing foghorn,
And could see the path no more.
The writhing grey monster approached now,
She took her shells and fled.
The whirling, hurling sea surged on,
And terrible thoughts went through her head.

Cherry looked back, the wave was there,
There was nothing more she could do,
But she clutched her shells against her chest,
And that was the last she knew.

Anthony Collins (11)
Locks Heath Junior School

HARVEST TIME

The ploughed brown fields,
The rain and sun,
The green, red, yellow apples
We get all of these at harvest time.

The tractor's ploughing,
The ripe fruit on the trees,
The autumn leaves blow across,
The ploughed brown fields.

I got the vegetable patch to pick carrots,
Potatoes, runner beans, swedes,
The autumn wind blows
The pears off the trees.

The golden wheat blowing in the fields,
My father gets ready to harvest the wheat
While I go and pick sweet peas
And the last of the tomatoes.

I also pick the mushrooms,
My father's helper Jamie gets the van ready
To go to the market
And sell all the fruit and vegetables.

Now we have to wait
Another whole year
We save some of the pickings
So we can eat them for our tea!

Christopher Collins (10)
Marycourt School

Special Person

S omeone very, very special
P iece together my heart
E xciting games together
C aring and loving we wish
I ndependence on Earth together
A lways and forever more
L oving and caring always

P eace to the world
E verybody cares about you
R unning to put the past behind
S omeone will care some day
O n the other hand love them
N o one else will

James Tott (11)
Marycourt School

My Messy Bedroom

My messy bedroom is disgusting,
My messy bedroom needs adjusting,
My messy bedroom needs a clean,
My messy bedroom is a scream!

My messy bedroom has been cleaned,
My messy bedroom is a dream,
My messy bedroom is all straight,
My messy bedroom is no longer a state.

I like my messy bedroom messy.

Jamille Hogg (9)
Marycourt School

ANIMAL SOUNDS

Pigs go oink
Pigs go splash
And they splutter in their pig swill mash

Pigs go grunt
Pigs go munch
As they gobble up a yummy lunch

Pigs go hot
Pigs go squelch
They're very rude and often belch

Pigs go snort
Pigs go snuffle
While they enjoy eating truffle.

Charlotte Ireland (11)
Marycourt School

WHIRLPOOL

W ater rushing down into the sea, giant
H ole of water
I nhaling boats and ships
R ushing round and round
L eaving nothing behind
P ulls and pulls until it is satisfied
O n everything it sucks up
O ver the world it travels, at
L ast it has gone.

Jamie Chappell (10)
Marycourt School

The Burger Boy To His Babe

Come and live with me please, and be my lover
And I will impress you so much
I'll give you such a funky ring
And drive you off to Burger King.

We'll sit upon a soft settee
Watching rugger and footy
Eating crisps, the ones with curls
While on our TV are the Spice Girls.

We'll drive a Ford around the street
I will sweep you off your feet
We'll go to bed late every night
So please come and be my lover!

Lee Smith (10)
Marycourt School

Snowball

S now
N ever
O utwits hot
W ater
B ut
A lways
L ikes
L ovely cold.

Edward Cooper (10)
Marycourt School

Sorry I'm Late For School

Sorry I'm late Miss,
My mum took a wrong turning,
So we went to Hawaii.
First my mum went to the dock,
Then she went onto the ferry.
My mum didn't know she was on the ferry,
So we kept going to the airport.
The plane left at half past eight,
And we got there at nine.
We drove to some Hawaiian dancers,
They gave us some grass skirts,
And some flower necklaces.
Then we took the same route to the motorway,
And that's why I'm late for school.
Will you give me lines?

Scott Rodwell (10)
Marycourt School

Juicy Fruits

The angry apple is sick and sad.
The blazing banana has a bursting flavour.
The mighty mango is massive and mad.
The perfect plum wobbled around like a wombat.
The private pear passed out poor and sad.
The pinky peach is a pumping panther.
The clever cherry is mighty and mad.
The obedient orange is sad and mad.

Abby Fuller (9)
Marycourt School

Untitled

I remember being really angry when:
My friend came round and broke my toys.
I felt really angry, like drawing on the walls.
I remember being really ignored when:
Me and my family went to the zoo
And I felt really ignored because
My family hardly said a word to me.
I remember being really proud when:
I did all the washing and cleaning up.
My family were really proud with me.
My family made me a certificate and
A medal and were very pleased.

Yes, I certainly do remember.

Charlotte Nugent (8)
Marycourt School

Remembering

I remember being really guilty when:
I was little I stole a handful of toy Easter chicks.
I remember being really guilty when:
I kept on forgetting my school hat.

I remember being really sad when:
My dog died.
I remember being really sad when:
Me and my mum were cleaning out my hamster's cage
And he leapt on to the floor and my mum picked him up
And accidentally dropped him.

Yes, I certainly do remember!

Emily Murray (8)
Marycourt School

UNTITLED

I felt annoyed when I went to Fairthorne Manor
because I kept getting stung by nettles.

I felt angry when we moved house
and we were looking for my book
and when we found the box with boys' books
written on it, it was full of Tupperware.

I felt sick when I went in a witch's cabin
because a man was holding a lady's head.

I felt a pain when I did a belly flop
off a high diving board into the pool.

Yes, I certainly do remember.

Richard Fulton (7)
Marycourt School

RIVERS

R ivers rush, rivers tumble,
I love rivers when they rumble,
V ery fast, very slow,
E very river always on the go,
R ushing rivers, tumbling rivers, very fast, very slow.

Charlotte Straw (10)
Marycourt School

GOING TO BED

Last night after supper,
I was a sucker.
My mother said,
Go to bed.

I went upstairs,
Got totally bare.
I couldn't find my pyjamas,
Given to me by farmers.

I went downstairs,
Still totally bare.
Everyone laughed,
I felt a draught.

I found my pyjamas,
Given to me by farmers.
I went to bed,
Totally red.

I hope tomorrow night,
While I watch the fight.
The thought of going to bed,
Doesn't come into my mother's head.

I pulled my cover up,
And knocked my cup.
It fell on the floor,
I gave out a roar.

I had a small cry,
Then shut my eyes.
In two seconds flat,
I was asleep like a run-over rat.

Gary Over (11)
Meadowland Junior School

SPACE

Up, up, away out there stars are spread
Shining like lights making the night sky seem magical.

Planets dancing round the sun
Giving us light and warmth
So flowers can grow and when there is snow
It melts it when it shines.

The moon is like a face guarding the Earth
Making sure it's safe at night
So when you're having nightmares
There is no need to fear 'cos
The light guard in the sky is very, very near.

There are lots and lots of planets
In the dark sky up above
Jupiter, Pluto, Venus, Earth and Mars.

More are to be found
Out among the stars and the hurling rocks
Zooming around the solar system.

Claire Caminada (10)
Milford Primary School

SPACE MISSION

Once I saw an astronaut gliding here and there,
Burning off the rocks and stones in the moonlit air.
Once I saw a meteor gliding here and there,
Shooting at the stars and planets missing every chance.
Once I saw a shooting star gliding here and there,
Swishing and darting everywhere, lighting up the atmosphere.

Benjamin Burgess (10)
Milford Primary School

CAPTURED

I was captured by aliens
And taken to Mars,
They locked me in a cell
With laser bars.
We flew across the Milky Way,
I had to eat straw and hay.
Their heads looked like rugby balls,
Their feet smelt of smelly tools.
They shoved me in a box
Full of smelly socks.
I landed in a tree,
I was stung by a bee.
When I got home
I found out my family had
Turned into aliens.
Ahhhhh!

Rebecca Hall (11)
Milford Primary School

ALIEN

I met an alien face to face
Who said he came from outer space
I listened to his story
And he said he was worshipped in glory
He flew around the Milky Way
And said to the folk there 'I'm sorry I can't stay'
I'd like to find outer space
And if I did I'd find a place
To stay with him in outer space
It would be great, it would be just ace!

Alana Lunn (10)
Milford Primary School

The Black Thing Outside Our Planet Called Space

Sounds are eerie up in space
But each sound has its own place
Sounds have all kinds of different sources
But up there, there aren't any forces
Up in space

Mars, Earth, Jupiter, Saturn
Up in space there is a pattern
Of the planets orbiting the sun
Learning about them is very fun
Up in space

Up there is a black hole
Putting things inside itself just like a bowl
Zooming asteroids and gas ball stars
Flying around a planet like Mars
Up in space.

Space is a wonderful place
It's full of things to do
And little secret places that I can take you to
The stars and planets are giving up a great chase
For dawn has broken.

Eleanor Darley (9)
Milford Primary School

Amazing Space

Planets floating on their own,
Frothing Venus full of foam.
They look like blobs of inky pen,
But were not meant for flying men.

The only lights in space are stars,
Lighting planets up, like Mars.
Each star looks like a firefly,
Giving joy to passers-by.

Nathalie Kealy (11)
Milford Primary School

THE SEARCH FOR AN ALIEN

We're going to stay at a space station,
What will it be like?
Will we have to ride in a space cart,
Or can I ride my bike?

What if I see an alien?
What will he say to me?
Will he say 'Hello'
Or will he say 'My name's Lee?'

So I went searching for an alien,
And then I saw a glimpse of green.
But when I went closer,
The alien had been seen!

He had a green head,
Blue body,
A million eyes,
And a name called Poddy.

So Poddy and I
Went back to the station,
Where I found my mum and dad
Looking at Poddy and I in anticipation.

Harriet James (10)
Milford Primary School

What If Space?

What if space
had no planets or stars
no Jupiter, sun
no moon or no Mars?

What a boring old thing
the night sky would be
with nothing to do
or nothing to see.

What if in space
a UFO was seen?
I'll shout and I'll shiver
'Look out' I'll scream.

What if in space
the sun turned to goo
then we'll have a life looking at space
with just me and you.

Alex Hall (11)
Milford Primary School

Space

In space there's lots of shooting stars
And sometimes they land on planet Mars
I flew to the moon
And there was a ship
That looked like a giant spoon
I met an alien called Moggie
And his cat was called Oggie
On my way home
I saw a crystal dome.

Emma Wright (10)
Milford Primary School

SPACE

Space, the moon, 1 planet, galaxies
Space, a big, big blackboard
Stars made out of gas in the moonlight
Pluto and Jupiter we can see in a telescope
Asteroids going here and there
A shooting star faster than a rocket
Ohh, space a wonderful place!

Oliver Wilkins (10)
Milford Primary School

SPACE

Space is big.
Planets everywhere.
Aliens could be living out there.
Comets and shooting stars, they are everywhere.
Shooting stars are whizzing past.
Oh how I wish I could live up there,
Floating without a care.

Danny Herd (10)
Milford Primary School

SATURN

S is for space shuttles.
A is for aliens who come to invade.
T is for Taurus, a constellation of stars.
U is for Uranus, a planet in the sky.
R is for the ringed stars.
N is for Neptune, another world that
moves around the stars.

Marissa Harvey (9)
Milford Primary School

Vast Empty Space

Drifting about in empty space,
Planets like overgrown *marbles.*
Wrapped and smothered all over in darkness,
The atmosphere *chilling* and airless.

Shimmering, glistening stars that are endless,
Radiant sun, *overpowering.*
Orian the powerful hunter, seems huge now!
And over there look, there's the Plough.

The moon all coated in giant, gaping craters,
Following closely in the wake of the Earth.
Venus swathed in a vast, *deadly,* death, cloud.
The one who created must be *extremely* proud!

Zoë Bargh (11)
Milford Primary School

Amazing Space

Up in space without a care,
Free and happy way up there.
Seeing all the planets that we learn about in school,
I wonder whether aliens live here at all?
I travel on the shooting stars,
Stopping off at the peaceful Mars.
Steering clear of the sizzling sun,
Staying there wouldn't be much fun!
I pass all the comets, they look so bright,
And I realise I'm so tiny compared with this vast night.
I lie in my bed, thinking about space,
Remembering my journey - it's a wonderful place.

Lucy Maule (10)
Milford Primary School

Can I See A Meteor

Can I see a meteor?
Flying up so high
Can I see a meteor?
In the moonlit sky.
Can I see a meteor?
Up there by the moon.
Can I see a meteor?
It will be out of sight soon.
Can I see a meteor?
It looks just like a pea.
No I can't see a meteor.
Can you not see?
I was dreaming about a meteor.
That just could not be!

Chris Conacher (11)
Milford Primary School

The Black Thing Called Space

Shooting stars flying over our heads,
Great mass of colours, silver and red,
Comets, asteroids zooming everywhere,
Spaceships and shuttles flying through the air,
But space isn't all fantasy and dreams,
People in space burst out in screams,
Because of black holes and aliens,
And spaceships they call failers,
So really as you can see,
Space just isn't the place for me!

Joanna Phillips (10)
Milford Primary School

Up In Space

Planets and the shooting stars,
Up in the very black, black sky.
Spaceships landing on the moon,
Space must be a very quite place.
Asteroids flying through the sky,
Everything floating all around.
Nobody lives there apart from the aliens,
But I don't think I'd like to go to space.

Louise Cobb (9)
Milford Primary School

UFO

Space the final frontier . . .
Put the ship in the highest gear!
Star Trek's coming right over here!
Put the ship in warp six!
I don't care if everyone's sick,
Fire torpedoes!
I bet they'll shoot, I suppose
Help! Help! Let's go on the run!
Oh no! We're heading to the *sun!*

Scott Smith (10)
Milford Primary School

All In Space

The stars look so high,
In the moonlit sky,
And then I say 'Oh my,'
Then I think, why?

You can't see the planets but I know there's nine,
Jupiter, Earth and mars, they're all mighty fine.
The blazing sun in space,
With the moon looking at its face.

David McAdam (11)
Milford Primary School

SPACE

What is out in space,
It is a very dark place,
Aliens fly in saucers,
Planning out routes and courses,
They have a mother ship,
I wonder if they have whips?
They have phasers,
Which look like lasers,
Aliens are out in space,
Although it's a very dark place.

Megan Butler (10)
Milford Primary School

PLANETS IN THE SKY

P is for Pluto, one of the planets,
L is for Leo, a cluster of stars,
A is for aliens who glide around in flying saucers,
N is for Neptune, another of the worlds
that move around the sun,
E is for Earth, the planet of life,
T is for Taurus, a constellation of stars,
S is for Saturn, the ringed planet.

Emma Olliff (9)
Milford Primary School

Space Is A Wonderful Place

I'd love it near my base
          I wish I could see Earth, Jupiter and Mars
I wish I could sit on the big shiny stars
          I wish I could see the Milky Way
It would really make my day!
          I wish I lived in space
It's such a wonderful place.

Aron Read (9)
Milford Primary School

Space

S hooting stars whizz.
P lanets orbit round and round.
A stronauts study the life of stars,
C ollecting data from Mars.
E arth is where us humans live
   and I hope we will be able for a long time to give.

Lucy Hockham (11)
Milford Primary School

Space

I wish I could go up in space
  Because it's just like my face.
    I wish I could sit on the stars
      And look down on my chocolate bars.
        Oh! That would be my perfect day.

Jonathan Daly (9)
Milford Primary School

MY LITTLE ALIEN FRIEND

My little alien friend
Will I ever see you again?
Up up away in space
Will you ever show your face?
Jupiter, Earth or Mars
Where do you live in the shooting stars?
What do you look like? Eight eyes?
With massive great feet big in size?
Maybe you're as small as an ant
Or as big as an elephant?
What can you do? Reach out for the Milky Way?
Or make cakes for the invaders who come and play?
Have you got a family?
What do they look like? Me?
My little alien friend, I really want to see!
For it's all a mystery!

Jasmine Caminada (10)
Milford Primary School

ALL GONE COSMIC!

C osmic is space, space is *ace!*
O f course it sounds all weird,
S huttles fly all around the place.
M y pet alien's got a beard.
I f we could go there for holidays
C an you guess how much we would have to get geared?

Joshua Bargh (9)
Milford Primary School

Space

I'd love to go up in space,
And meet an alien face to face.
I'd like to land on the moon and Mars,
Or even on some shooting stars.
I'd love to go up there at night,
Watching all the stars shine bright.
I'd like to visit the Milky Way,
I wonder what it's like to stay?
When I come home,
I'd tell my friends,
That I'd been to space,
And it's a marvellous place.

Lucy Read (10)
Milford Primary School

Space

If I could travel into space,
I would take a huge suitcase.
You never know what could be up there,
So I'm going to start to prepare.
If an alien with an ugly face,
Came up to me and said '*Get out of space!*'
I would kill him and take him home,
To put him in the garden disguised as a gnome!
I'd take him everywhere I go,
And put him in a museum to put on show.

Zoe Crawford (11)
Milford Primary School

Fantastic Space

Up, up and away in space,
It is an extraordinary place.
Jupiter, Earth, Sun and Mars,
Pluto, Neptune, Moon and stars.
People say there's aliens up there,
So if I went I'd have to take great care!
I'd like to ride on a shooting star,
And travel so very far.
Gleaming comets and a red hot sun,
If I went into space, I know I'd have fun.
At night when the moon shines silvery bright,
I think about space:
It's a wonderful sight.

Melanie Rocher (10)
Milford Primary School

One Night I Saw

One night I saw some stars,
I don't know why but they were circling Mars.
Next to it was a planet,
that looked like it was made from granite.
After that the sun came round,
looking like a bun with no sound.
Soon will come the moon,
and rockets with pockets will be flying.
But at the moment now,
there's nothing.
Nothing, not even a cow jumping over the moon,
or a dish running away with a spoon.

Ben Kett (9)
Milford Primary School

WHAT I SAID TO THE SNOW

Dear Snow

Why do you rush down so fast?
Is it because you're unhappy?
Why are you so cold and icy?
You are not so bold.
Why do you twinkle?
You aren't very bright,
But do you shine in the moonlight?
You're lovely when you sparkle,
But you roar like a boar.
Who is the person that you hate?
Is it the people who slam the gate?
Is it me or is it he?
Please tell me anyway
On a lovely Christmas Day.

Emma Joseph (9)
Milford Primary School

WHAT I SAID TO THE SNOW

Dear Snow

Make children happy on Christmas Day.
On Christmas Day the children wake up and see you falling.
Silently you fall in lovely patterns.
When the children get up and get dressed, the ski lift starts.
Snowboards, skis and ski schools go up on the lift and have a wonderful day.
Snow, oh snow, you make everybody happy.
Thank you so much.

Jennifer Keeping (8)
Milford Primary School

WHAT I SAID TO THE SNOW

Dear Snow,

You are so cold.
You are fun to play with.
Your soft snowflakes tickle me.
You go with the blizzard.
You drift away happily.
You leave so fast.
You are so lonely when you come to my house.
You are desperate to stay.
Oh bother! You're leaving.
Goodbye snow. See you next year.

Matthew Theobald (8)
Milford Primary School

WHAT I SAID TO THE RAIN

Dear Rain,

Why do you rain down so heavily?
Why do you drizzle so lightly?
Why do you rain water instead of Panda pop?
Why are you called rain?
Why is your water so salty?
So many questions to answer,
So hurry, hurry and answer them all,
Before I give you more!

Amy Dyson (9)
Milford Primary School

What I Said To The Snow

Dear Snow

How you fall so gently,
Giving joy to all mankind,
Covering this and covering that,
Oh how we all shout *hurrah*,
When you fall on cars and trees.
But sometimes you become a blizzard,
Flooding the Earth in snow,
Falling angrily,
Lashings of snow.
Oh please, be a nice gentle snow.

Calum Harris (8)
Milford Primary School

What I Said To The Rain

Dear Rain,

Why do you make puddles?
Why do you drop rain on us?
Why do you dribble and why are you so silly?
Why do you make people cold?
Why do you bother me?
Why do you drop rain on me?
Why do you make noises
and drop rain on our houses at night?
Why do you make the wind so angry?

Goodbye rain.

Rebecca Woolgar (9)
Milford Primary School

What I Said To The Rain

Dear Rain

Why do you roar your storms at us
Why do you rain on Sunday morning
Why do you come raging at us
Why do you bring the children nightmares
Why do you flood the little villages
Why do you not come in the desert
Why do you not mind when we need you too?
You will not get any friends the way you are doing things.
Why are you so desperate?

Sam Shepherd (9)
Milford Primary School

What I Said To The Snow

Dear Snow

Why do you fall so heavily
and cover all the ground?
Covering everything with your
frosty flakes that happen to be around.
Why do you freeze the children
and turn their toes to frost?
Why does the horrible frosty snow
cover all the world?

Chloe Wallis (8)
Milford Primary School

Blizzard

Oh! Stop that howling blizzard.
Oh! Stop all that coldness and bitterness.
Oh! Be still and calm and quiet.
Oh! Stop drifting the snow towards us.
Oh! Stop coming to us on Christmas Day.
Be happy. Be friendly.
Make us happy and then we will like you.

Katherine Fournier (9)
Milford Primary School

The Wind

The wind moves kites.
The wind is cold.
The wind blows very strongly when it wants.
The wind cries very quietly.
The wind whooshes round the bend.
The wind blows the leaves.

Jon Clark (7)
Milford Primary School

The Rain

Pitter-patter goes the rain.
Cold, sad, tinkling all day.
Drip, drop, what's that coming from the sky?
Oh no, not the rain again!
Yippee! It's gone, that terrible rain.
Oh stop being so miserable.

Michael Kealy (7)
Milford Primary School

The Earth

The Earth is a small,
pretty marble,
Kept on a cloth of
darkness.
There are lots of
marbles like him,
Some red, some golden,
some darker.

It's nice to watch them
rolling,
Over the black velvet
cloth,
Watching the planets
mixing,
Like colours in a
paint pot.

Megan Baynham (11)
Orchard Junior School

Earth

The Earth is a giant marble.
It rolls round,
lit up by a yellow sun.
When it's dark it has no colour.
The game is over,
the dark has won!

Michael Naidoo (11)
Orchard Junior School

SPACE

The Earth is a spaceship
stuck in gear, moving round the sun.
Pluto is a planet of ice
freezing anything that comes near.
Planets whizzing about
like aliens in a hurry.
Sunbeams shooting out of those planets
until one big meteor charges at the Earth.
It misses and hits the sun.
The sun starts to fall, then darkness.
Space has been camouflaged in its natural colour.
In the night you can see
those little spaceships shining.

Daniel Humphries (11)
Orchard Junior School

THE EARTH AT NIGHT

The Earth at night is a patchwork quilt
of blues and greens, and a faint neon glow.
The blue is a calm sea of velvet
and the green a rough terrain of sacking.
The people down far below
desert the winding streets
as all the stars look down on Earth
and see a wondrous sight.
The Earth at night is a patchwork quilt
made with the finest needles.
Gently lit by the moon
as it watches the miracle
that has been created.

Matthew Irwin (10)
Orchard Junior School

The Sun Is A Golden Ship

The sun is a golden ship,
glinting in the sun,
with sails of gold
and solid brass decks
rushing past the day sky.

As the day grows old,
clouds finger the sky
like the newborn fog
on the cold horizon
down on planet Earth.

When night has come
and the ship is sunk,
when gold has turned to dust,
our sun has gone around the world
and does so every night.

Ben McMonagle (10)
Orchard Junior School

The Apple

Earth is a rosy crisp apple
spinning round and round,
into winter, spring, summer and autumn.
Winter's fog wraps around the apple
like a blanket of grey,
Spring's showers are the apple's juice
trickling down its edge,
Summer's sun is a ball of fire
dripping over the apple's surface,
Clouds of mist envelop the apple in autumn.

Catherine Smith (11)
Orchard Junior School

Marble Of The Stars

The Earth is the best
In God's marble collection
Out of reds and blues and greens
Earth is His prize
His absolute winner
He loves it with all His heart
And the people are happy
Until . . .
They forget to smile
Then pollution, famine, war!
So whether you want the Earth
To be black, not green
Remember God has other marbles
And Earth won't always be the best.

Sarah Harding (11)
Orchard Junior School

Space

From my spaceship I can see,
The Earth, twisting around in space
like a ball.
The sea, a calm, blue, flat sheet.
The people, clusters of them,
standing like a forest of trees.
The land, a green, bumpy mass.
The stars, jewels twinkling.
The planets, balls of colours, floating.
The sun, a round ball of fire.
The moon, a shiny beast of the night.

Stephanie Day (11)
Orchard Junior School

EARTH

Earth is a bubble floating in the universe,
Watching the golden doves flying around a blanket
of black velvet,
Floating through puffs of white cotton wool,
The golden sun falls asleep on a puff of smoke
from a dragon's nose,
The bubble continues to spin round and round in
the darkness,
The moon comes to play,
he swims around islands in the black sea,
The bubble chases with the moon, but never seems
to catch it,
Until *pop* lightning has burst the bubble,
all is quiet.

Rebecca Wooldridge (10)
Orchard Junior School

COSMIC

The Earth is a god living in space
With Pluto his dog, a pet,
Milky Way, a chocolate long lace,
He sees night and day.
Night is space, not a time to play,
Day is sun and a time to play.
People are toys, his plastic soldiers,
A game of life who decides who wins or loses?
The moon his mirror at night.
Can you think where his house is?

Jennifer McKnight (11)
Orchard Junior School

THE FRUIT BOWL OF PLANETS

The Earth is a giant succulent orange as it turns
around in the fruit bowl of planets,
The glow of the yellow grapefruit
shining down upon it,
Gravity stops the orange from flying out of the bowl
and into space,
The crescent banana is the moon hiding one side
from the spinning orange,
The twenty-four segments of the orange represent
every hour from dawn to dawn,
Just think, the universe which holds all these planets
could be on your table right now!

Colette Pain (10)
Orchard Junior School

EARTH

The Earth is a bubble floating amongst millions of others
in a pitch-black room.
A ball of light shines on different sides of it, as it drifts past.
Some are *big*, some are *small*
but all fly together in the darkness.
If you looked closely over hundreds of years ago
you would have seen the Earth as the most beautiful orb ever,
reflecting brilliant colours and shades.
But if you look now,
you will see the Earth turning into a hideous ball of pollution and gas.
If you are not careful,
this world may come to a horrible end.

Sophie Colverson (11)
Orchard Junior School

EARTH

The Earth is a swamp
Sunken treasures buried in the sunken islands
Dead and spoilt by disease and litter
All this rubbish is everywhere
Shopping trolleys all dismantled by decaying times
Just one has survived it all, it's by one man who's
Living in a dream, he's just polishing them again and
again living off his own flesh and blood
(Richard, Richard wake up!)
I'm awake now, I was only dreaming, soon not to be
not just a dream but a sad end to the world that once
was blue and green, but soon to be a horrid greenish
slime.

Richard Brooks (11)
Orchard Junior School

EARTH

The bubble was floating, up and up it rose,
Higher and higher, higher than the floating
black world,
The bubble kept going till it reached the
skies of darkness,
Where it entered the world in front,
So when the bubble saw the sun, the sun
got really angry,
The sun was heating up, trying to pop the
bubble,
But when the bubble spun around the exit
was gone!

Fiona Bennett (10)
Orchard Junior School

EARTH

The Earth is a rolling bouncy ball,
rolling around a netball sun.
Rolling on a velvet cloth that turns blue and black.
When the cloth is black there are thousands of waving hands.
The bouncy ball twists and twists, but never stops
like an ever-spinning top.

Other bouncy balls are spinning too,
every colour you can imagine,
any size, any shape.
Some are playing hula-hoop,
some are on their own.
At night lots of tiny red balls
put on a spectacular show,
whizzing around the cloth,
leaving a trail all around.

Every time the cloth is black,
this show is put on
and every time the waving hands
applaud quietly so no one can hear.

Rebecca Joyce (11)
Orchard Junior School

EARTH

The Earth is a bubble
floating around in space,
just spinning here
and spinning there,
just waiting for its fate.

All of a sudden a meteor,
just as if it was a pin,
for Earth it is in trouble.
Pop! The meteor hit.
There is no more sweet Earth.

Peter Burden (10)
Orchard Junior School

Cosmic

Far away out of sight,
beyond the stars there shines a light.
Throughout the years it always glows,
from where it comes, no one knows.
Could it be the burning sun
or a raybeam from Captain Cosmic's gun.

Jordan Heathorn (8)
Park Gate Primary School

Cosmic

Hedgehogs snuffling through the bushes
counting all of them, one, two, three,
asleep in the light and awake in the dark.
Hedgehogs shiny, black noses sniffing in
the air looking for food.
Little paws scurrying along, soon it will be light
once again the little hedgehogs will go back
into sleep for the day and come out again.

Rachel Browne (9)
Park Gate Primary School

Cosmic

Cosmic is good
Cosmic is fun
Aliens go up and rest on the sun.

Cosmic is good
Cosmic is fun
People go up and have some fun.

Jennifer Hurst (9)
Park Gate Primary School

Surfing The Galaxy

I wish I could go and see the moon
And eat up all the cheese,
I wish I could go to Pluto
And feel the blowing breeze,
I wish I could go and see the sun
I've heard it's very hot,
I wish I could go to Jupiter
And see the bright red spot.

Tasmine Ash-Cutler (10)
Ridgemede Junior School

JULY TO NOVEMBER

In July it's Father's Day,
So be kind to your dad.
Try to make him feel good
Don't try to make him sad.

August is a lovely month,
All the leaves go brown,
They fall off the trees,
In the strong, strong breeze,
That blows them into town.

In September it's back to school,
I'm going to fill my brain.
Oh no! A dark cloud is coming!
I think it's going to rain!

It's scary in October,
Because it's Hallowe'en.
There is no place more scary,
That I have ever seen.

In November we have fireworks,
And put on special shows.
Then I get my hanky out
And blow my runny nose!

Daniel Conneely (8)
Rowner Junior School

PEACE

Peace in the playground
Peace at home
Peace in the church
Peace when you're asleep

Peace in the playground
My best friend
Boys playing football
Boo, boo, boo goes the girls

Peace at home
Peace in the church
Peace when you're asleep

Peace at home
In your bedroom
Listening to your music
All day long

Peace in the church
Peace when you're asleep

Peace in the church
People are praying
So, so quiet
That's the church

Peace when you're asleep

Peace when you're asleep
Thank goodness for that
Sister not screaming

Peace in the playground
Peace at home
Peace in the church
Peace when you're asleep.

Joanne Hallett (10)
St Monica Junior School, Southampton

GYMNASTICS

Vault.

First you run up hard
Jump on the springboard
Make sure your hands get on!
Over your feet go
Kick your heels up
You'll get over just fine
Then you land it
Phew, it's all over.

Bars.

Gentle swing through
'Pull your trousers up,' they say
On no, I'm up on the bar
Kick your feet high
Put your feet on the bar
Catch the high bar
Swing, swing as high as you can
Pull your trousers up again
Kick your feet high
Swing through
Doing a back somersault.

Gemma Thomas (10)
St Monica Junior School, Southampton

Peace At Last

As I walk through the wood
My head under my hood
I wish I was home in the warm
With the fire and snow-covered lawn.

I come to my door, slip in the key
And turn it round and round and round.
Through the door I bound,
I hear an argument raging
All about cleaning and wages.
I creep to my room
I have the feeling of doom.

He storms out slamming the door
She shouts and yells some more.
I hide,
For I can not abide these horrid arguments.

When I venture out,
The argument is nowt,
They are sitting on the sofa with a glass of wine
Talking about going out to an expensive place to dine.

I make myself some dinner
Because I'm sure I'm getting thinner
I'm writing in my diary
Trying to describe the argument in great detail,
But it doesn't seem to make sense
So instead I just put
Peace at last!

Kirsty Gibbon (11)
St Monica Junior School, Southampton

Four Seasons By The Sea

In the summer by the sea
the waves are small.
The sea is calm and
people are getting suntans.

In the autumn by the sea
the waves get a little
bit bigger and the wind begins
to blow.

In the winter by the sea
it's a complete change,
waves are crashing
against the rocks.

In the spring by the sea
once again a big change
it's calm but not as still
as summer.

Marie Ballard (11)
St Monica Junior School, Southampton

Lonely

Lonely, I felt like a night without stars,
A field without corn,
I didn't like it, I'm sure you won't too.
The world seemed a dreadful place,
Being lonely I do regret.
Being lonely I will not forget.

Joseph Connelly (8)
St Monica Junior School, Southampton

The Old Tree

A reddy brown, wrinkly tree standing in a wood,
With red and yellow leaves swaying in the breeze,
With people dancing around it.
People singing,
Children looking at me,
With squirrels crawling in my hair.
I just can't stand it.
My hand-shaped leaves scare people in the night,
And in the night children climb on me
And hurt my bark.
My leaves are green, red, yellow, brown, and
I do not like my leaves because they frighten me at night.
People used to come and look at me
But now they don't.

Natalie Diaper (8)
St Monica Junior School, Southampton

Pollution In The Fish Pond

His mother's dead, he cannot swim
Due to what's on top of him.
There are no plants, he cannot breathe,
He has to force himself to heave.
He cannot go, he cannot stay
He has to be like this all day.
Can of Coke, can of beans,
He will never reach his teens.
He will never jump and play,
He will always be this way.
He can't get out, he will not try
For he knows he has to die.

Laura Paine (11)
St Monica Junior School, Southampton

My Life

When I grow up
I'm going to get a baby pup
And I'll travel far
Like a shooting star
And I'll turn around
And be given a crown
I'll work in chip shops
Selling lollipops
I'll shop and shop
Till I drop
I'll work on ships
Eating orange pips
I'll eat a cherry pie
Then I'll soon die.

Hannah Jewell (11)
St Monica Junior School, Southampton

The Sea

Smooth, peaceful, white waves
washing on your feet.
Calm, soft, still, so relaxed.
Spray flung, gentle breeze
birds singing.
But it can all change
wild, stormy, harsh, rough
A hazard waiting to happen
fierce, savage, ferocious, cruel
waves crashing, boats sinking,
rocks tumbling.

Anne-Marie Wakeford (11)
St Monica Junior School, Southampton

THE CHANGING SEAS

The furious waves collided against the sand,
Lightning struck, the wind wailed.
The thunder boomed a severe pattern,
Stormy waves smashed against the bare rocks.

Slowly but surely the sun glistened,
The waves stopped rolling, the wind listened.
The rain was spitting, the sun was gleaming,
Then a beautiful rainbow appeared.

I could see ships in the distance,
They were recovering from the gale.
The seagulls were squawking
Picking fish at their delight,
All of the children came down to the sea once more.

Michael Matthews & Andrew Deakin (11)
St Monica Junior School, Southampton

A THUNDEROUS STORM!

As I stared at the tempest waves.
The wind was shouting with a rave.
I could feel the white spray from the sky.
A shiver rushed down my back, *why?*

Back back the water ran.
Causing much abuse.
Unbearable wind, destroying everything
Felt like a hurricane fierce and rough.

Suddenly brightness filled the air.
Light was all around.
I let myself fall back and enjoyed the peaceful sun.

Rebecca Millington (10)
St Monica Junior School, Southampton

My Monster

I have a monster in my car.
It is bigger than me by far,
He eats scraps, he drinks tar.
I found him in a jar,
Without his Ma or Pa.

He used to be the monster king,
I don't know how he could be that thing.
He's got a good voice and he likes to sing,
And he's got stubby fingers and a gorgeous gold ring.

He ran away,
On a rainy day,
He passed away and I didn't know what to say,
I was sad that day
Because the monster passed away.

Jamie Lamacraft (11)
St Monica Junior School, Southampton

Storm From Day To Dusk

The early morning crashing ocean,
a thunderous thunderstorm blows over the sea.
Quick as a cheetah the lightning crashes,
hits the water with tremendous splashes.

The mighty thunder, loud as a drum,
white water froth curling into the waves
hits the shore with the crackle of pebbles.

The waves calm down, the thunderstorm dies,
the night appears as the flaky moon sprinkles
over the horizon.

Darren Morris (11)
St Monica Junior School, Southampton

The Pound Dog

There once was a boy
Who lived underground
He had a dog
That spat out a pound
Then one day
The dog saw a bitch
He spat up some more
And then they were rich.

They got a new car
A Vauxhall Cavalier
Then he went mad
And drove off a pier
They both nearly drowned
But the dog spat up a pound
And broke the glass
So they swam to the grass.

Philip Wilson (11)
St Monica Junior School, Southampton

My Best Friend In Orbit

My best friend went into space,
His rocket went at a steady pace.
All because I said, 'Get off my case.'
Now I'm starting to regret it.

He's probably being a Martian King,
Eating some disgusting thing.
All my friends are starting to sing,
So please, please come back.

Your mother is very sad,
Your father is very mad,
Your brother is a kind lad,
And I will forgive you.

If you do not come back,
Can I have your rucksack?
There is one thing that you may lack
A good source of gravity.

Leah Manley (11)
St Monica Junior School, Southampton

A Thunderous Rage

As I stared at the tempest waves
A ferocious gale clashed with my umbrella and nearly blew me away!
We could hear violent waves colliding across the rocks
And the slapping just approaching us.
Back, back the water goes
Causing much abuse
Unbearable winds, destroying everything
It feels like a hurricane, fierce, rough and unpleasant.

Gigantic waves throwing over ships, rising to the clouds
I could feel the white spray from the darkening down, down sky
Suddenly brightness filled the air
Light was all around
I heard the seagulls scream with happiness
After all the storm was over
There was a gentle breeze brushing past my face, it was so quiet
I let myself fall back and enjoy the peaceful sun.

Claire Petley (10)
St Monica Junior School, Southampton

THE UNPREDICTABLE SEA

The wind is like a charging rhino
running out to sea
And the gigantic waves crash ashore
with tremendous strength.
Winds start howling like a ferocious dog
tossing the sea around, making violent waves.

Then all of a sudden it turned calm and quiet
all you could hear were the seagulls crying
The sea then looked like a sheet of glass
with just a gentle rippling on the surface.
The wind has died and all I can hear now is
a gentle whistle.

Paul Arthur (11)
St Monica Junior School, Southampton

GLASS BREAKER

We were by the sea on a restful day
The sea was pleasant and relaxed
It was as if it was glass
The air smelt like a fresh fragrance
Suddenly the sky exploded and turned black
Then the sea shattered into a thousand pieces.
We stood there watching as the sea revolved over onto
the sandy beach,
And listened to the seagulls crying in the background
Then there was a flash of lightning and we ran home in
the rain, thunder and lightning and we were safe once again.

Stephanie Pratt (11)
St Monica Junior School, Southampton

When I'm In The Sea

When I'm in the sea, the sea, the sea,
When I'm in the sea I see creatures great and small,
The swordfish boldly swims around with
his head always still,
for when I'm in the sea, I see creatures great
and small.

The pike is swimming, looking for food and
slyly finds his prey,
for when I'm in the sea, the sea, the sea,
for when I'm in the sea I see creatures great
and small.

There's fish swimming wildly as they hurry
to their mother,
for when I'm in the sea, the sea, the sea,
I see creatures great and small.

Lauren Miller (10)
St Monica Junior School, Southampton

The Storm Machine

Thunder struck, lightning flashed,
rumble, rumble, rumble.
Gate clanging, leaves falling,
rumble, rumble, rumble.
Tremendous boom from machine,
dog dived for the chair,
rumble, rumble, rumble.
Cogwheels turning, teeth churning,
ca boom . . . ca boom . . . ca boom!

Carly Boston (10)
St Monica Junior School, Southampton

The Vivid Sea

On the gorgeous gentle beach,
We sat watching the seagulls flying by,
Over the top of the gleaming sea.

The outstanding dazzling stillness
Suddenly broke into ripples,
Some boys were throwing stones
Trying to hit the seagulls.

We stood still, watching the ripples
Whither and fade,
Gradually the sea became relaxed and
Motionless once again.

Hannah Louise Scully & Chelsey Weeks (10)
St Monica Junior School, Southampton

The Wild Sea

Sway, sway, sway
I can hear the sea go by,
Whoosh, whoosh, whoosh,
The water up in the sea
The water is so salty, as salty as can be
But never mind.
The boats come down in the salty sea
Splash, splash, splash,
The boat is in the sea,
The fish in the sea
Can swim like a bee
Whoosh, whoosh, whoosh,
The water in the sea.

Sabrina Masterman (11)
St Monica Junior School, Southampton

THE SEA

The white water splashing against the ocean rocks,
Sand rolling gently, slowly over my feet.
Everyone playing games and people having a
relaxing swim.
Fish swimming out at sea,
Over and under the old ship wrecks.

The sun goes down and crowds go,
The moon comes out.
Whales come up for air,
The old pier closes,
Now the sea is quiet and the fish
get some sleep.

Sam Noble (10)
St Monica Junior School, Southampton

LONELY

Lonely, lonely I am
From my friends
Picking on me
My friends go off
I don't know where to go
The plants look dull
I am very lonely
Hated by my friends
Who won't let me play
Won't be nice to me
I am lonely like a lonely tree in a field.

Matthew Wilson (9)
St Monica Junior School, Southampton

BY THE SEASIDE

We walk down to the sea today
to see the lovely, smooth, clear, gentle, still sea
coming against our feet.
We watch the sea flowing
so calmly as the peaceful waves
come against us.
When we stand near the sea our feet
sink into the wet, slimy sand.
As the sun dies down and the waves
die down, we walk home with wet feet.

Sarah Dyer & Sarah C (11)
St Monica Junior School, Southampton

THE SCARY POEM

It is kind of spooky in the woods.
The tree is like a monster,
Reaching out its branches,
Like fingers trying to grab me.
The leaves are falling,
They are red like blood.
It is squelchy on the ground.
I am touching the tree.
The bark is hard and hurting my hand.

Garry Hasler (8)
St Monica Junior School, Southampton

THE BEACH

At the beach you can hear the
waves crashing onto the rocks
The sea tastes like salt
The sand is hot on your feet
it feels smooth and soft

You can hear the children playing
and making sandcastles
The wind in your face is cold
and dry, people swimming in the sea
People playing with their rubber
rings having such fun.

Lisa Verge (11)
St Monica Junior School, Southampton

LONELY

Of all the days, today's the worst,
In lessons you *dread* playtime,
Out in the playground you've found a bench,
Then some boys come and shove you off,
So you just end up standing around,
Oh I hate being lonely,
It feels
Like a bottomless pit falling down, down,
Through the middle of the earth.

Lana Gibbon (9)
St Monica Junior School, Southampton

THE GIANT

In the woods is a giant.
It has a hundred hands.
The leaves swish in the dark night.
It has roots for legs.
The hands are loose.
The red tree-blood can't come out
Or else the giant will die.

Ian Haythorne (7)
St Monica Junior School, Southampton

WHY AM I ALONE?

As I sat and watched my friends desert me,
I felt really empty inside.
Alone with my thoughts and feelings,
Nobody to share them with or to like me.
Why has everyone got friends except me?
What has everyone got that I haven't?
Is it the trainers?
Or the parents?
What is it?
And why is it always me?
Why am I alone?

Zöe Burns (9)
St Monica Junior School, Southampton

LONELY

I'm the loneliest girl on Earth
The loneliest
I feel like I'm in a dark cave on my own
Because my friends do not like me
They hang around with my worst enemy
I don't know why
Tell me why God
Tell me why
If I was a fish in the sea
I would be the only fish in the sea
That's how I feel.

Kirsty Hawkins (9)
St Monica Junior School, Southampton

THE GROWING TREE

In squishy wet ground
Some roots are growing
Going upwards
You will see sap in a hole
A few rustling leaves
The wind is blowing
Look! Some eyes watching
Its lined bark
The fingers are nearly
Touching the sky.

Sofala Stokes (7)
St Monica Junior School, Southampton

AN OLD BEGGAR

An old man sits outside,
waiting for people to come by.
He wears rags and no shoes,
and he wears a ripped hat.
With a dirty face he looks at me,
as he is supposed to do.
He looks sad with no money as he begs for money
with his hat,
and with a sad face he turns round and looks at me again.
He sleeps on the floor with other cats scratching off their fleas.
He can't have a shower, he is poor and lives on the floor.
He cries at night and prays to God that he will get a few
pence the next day.

Sofi Pascual (10)
St Patrick's Junior School, Woolston

THE VOICE OF AUTUMN

As I take over and get
summer out of my way,
I see little squirrels scattering
around collecting their acorns.
Golden brown crispy leaves
falling down onto the
hard concrete floor.
Conkers hanging off branches
ready to fall.
Then the whistling wind
whooshes them off as they
fall onto the hard ground.
Days are getting shorter,
nights are getting longer,
icy winds and dew on the grass.
Now I go and winter pushes me
out of the way.

Kerry Broomfield (11)
St Patrick's Junior School, Woolston

THE BEGGARMAN

The poor old man scuffs his feet
as he sadly walks along the street
He sits in a cramped, smelly shelter
with just a carrier bag for a home.

The poor old man with a bag
for an outdoor home
Nowhere to live or stay
just on his own in the middle of nowhere

The poor old man sits with
a battered felt hat
Hanging by the tips of his
fingers shaking madly

It's getting dark, now he's walking
on down the alleyway
Where's he gone
the poor old beggarman.

Mary Townsend-Rose (10)
St Patrick's Junior School, Woolston

All Hallows Eve

On my broom I quietly wait,
To see the zombies slowly wake.

In the graveyard noises here and there,
There are vampires, ghouls and ghosts, so *beware!*

Children knocking on doors saying 'Trick or treat,'
Vampire likes children, he thinks they are neat.

Come back you one-eyed cats
To see the werewolves, witches and bats.

Beware,
You're
In
For a
Scare
on Hallowe'en Night
Tu-whit tu-whoo.

Claire Malone (11)
St Patrick's Junior School, Woolston

THE DEVIL'S DREAM

Dead-eyed cats limping all around with Satan sat
in the smoky underground.

Hell as red as done murderous zombies going to come . . .

Ghouls grabbing you round the neck as you scream
heck, heck, heck . . .

Dogs spying on you through the fence as
they look at you quiet and dense.

As the flickering flames of hell die down,
it turns to a day of *nightmares* with the . . .

Devil's Crown.

Michael Lee (11)
St Patrick's Junior School, Woolston

ICE-CREAM

Tongue-tangling,
Mouth-watering,
Lip-smacking,
Tonsil-slaughtering,

White as snow,
Watch it go,

In my mouth,
Down south,

'This is lovely!' I said on my last lick,
'Oh no!' I groaned, 'now I feel sick!'

Keith Malecki (10)
St Patrick's Junior School, Woolston

AUTUMN

It's the autumn time,
Come for fun,
Until it's bedtime 'Hardly, Mum,'
The hibernating animals are all in their
Warm homes,
While the leaves fall down
And rustle on the ground.

Lilly-Anne Young (10)
St Patrick's Junior School, Woolston

HALLOWE'EN

Pitch black night,
unwanted shadows,
witches terrible as ever,
terrible yellow teeth and claws,
spotty as well,
howling wolves, witches cackling, *Ha! Ha! Ha!*

Charlotte Paull-Chorley (10)
St Patrick's Junior School, Woolston

AUTUMN

Misty mornings, it must be autumn,
A carpet of red, brown, yellow fragile leaves,
Golden fruits and fruits that turn bright red like apples,
Dew damp grass,
Scrambling for conkers,
Gloomy thoughts of winter cheered as Hallowe'en's coming,
I can't wait until the snow comes.

Carrie Lee (10)
St Patrick's Junior School, Woolston

A POEM FOR CHRISTMAS

Christmas bells ringing,
Carol singers singing.
Oh dear I should be asleep, he's here!
Father Christmas is here.

Drinking his beer,
Rudolf is here.
Bringing Christmas cheer,
Wrappers on the floor.
Quick open the door,
My Nan's here.

Christmas cards hanging,
Crackers are banging.
Santa comes with lots of toys
Because we've been good girls and boys.

Daniel Baker (10)
St Patrick's Junior School, Woolston

HALLOWE'EN!

Ahhh! I heard it in the distance as I pulled the cover over me.
I hate Hallowe'en, it's the scariest day of the year.
I hear the creaking of a skeleton getting blown away.
Vampires rising from their coffins.
I look out of the window, I see a black figure flying past
It comes to the window, its hat flew off and it was a witch,
Then it flew away, I pulled the cover up over me and
Peeked out a bit, it turned 1.00am and it all went dead.
It's the next day and I'm glad!

Shaun Farmer (11)
St Patrick's Junior School, Woolston

All Soul's Night

Vampires with teeth of red,
are found among their coffin bed.

Witches cackle in the pale moonlight,
ghouls and ghosts are in full flight.

Door to door, trick or treating,
witches, goblins, talking, meeting.

Lanterns, pumpkins with orange skin,
fantasies run wild within.

Shrieks and screams from far away,
The Hallowe'en gang's come to play!

Rosie O'Sullivan (11)
St Patrick's Junior School, Woolston

Lydia At Ten Months Old

She plays jokes on me
Bites my toes
Teases me, shouts at me
Wakes me up in the morning
Runs after me when I'm going somewhere
Crawls up the stairs
Falls down the stairs
She gets mad when I take something of hers
She laughs at me when I get told off.

That's my sister
at ten
months
old.

Lewis Rosario (10)
St Patrick's Junior School, Woolston

The Ballad Of The Mystic Rose

The mystic rose was shining
Outside the castle's gates
Inside was a king who was dying
That was his fate
He was told by a sign not to touch the rose
But the king did not listen
He went up to smell the rose but he touched it with his nose

But this was not the first time
A pretty maid had done it before
Everybody was upset
When they found her lying on the floor

They built a castle to remember the maid
Everyone in the land helped
They built the castle exactly where she laid
And above the mystic rose
The word 'Beware' stayed.

Thomas Gregory (10)
St Patrick's Junior School, Woolston

Listen

I'm walking through a place where
there's lots of apple trees,
I listen, I hear my feet walking on the
bright short green grass.

The sun is shining on my head
I find some shade,
I sat down by a nearby tree and
hear a little stream wash by.

The stream is cold and cool, I splash it
on my face, the clear water
sink beneath my hands, I listen, the breeze
sways the trees side to side.

The birds start chattering
they fly overhead,
I pick myself up and
walk on ahead.

Catherine Phillips (10)
St Patrick's Junior School, Woolston

RAIN

Wet, dull, gloomy day,
Rain, rain go away!

Window wipers on and off,
People walking by, cough, cough, cough!

Wet clothes! Wet hair,
Big umbrellas everywhere!

Dark clouds are forming,
Weather forecasts are warning!

Thunderbolts crashing,
Little children splashing.

Then the sun comes up, the rain dies down,
And all the people look up and frown!

Samantha Porter (11)
St Patrick's Junior School, Woolston

Ghouls And Ghosts

It's a dark and gloomy night,
when ghosts come out to fright.

Spiders crawling up and down,
bats flying round and round.

Pumpkin lanterns burn so bright,
and soon out goes the shining light.

Dead zombies rise from the ground,
amid a creepy chilling sound.

Hallows Eve is a real fright,
believe me, don't go out tonight.

Daniel Cansdale (11)
St Patrick's Junior School, Woolston

Satan's Little Helper

My master, (Satan) and I, (a ghoul)
Storming through
A dark and misty night.
He drops me into an empty zoo,
I climb through the gates and give someone a fright
My master bursts through the ground,
On a cold black chair.
Red rocks were thrown around,
As they crashed they gave off a glowing red glare.
I floated on a little bit more to give someone
Else a fright,
I was so pleased with myself I cackled with
Delight!

Craig Anderson (11)
St Patrick's Junior School, Woolston

AUTUMN JOURNEY

Here I come, come on summer, out the way,
I am here and here to stay.
I can make beautiful leaves fall off the trees,
crimson, gold and fiery red,
Hour by hour the day ticks away, the nights are longer
the days are shorter,
Suddenly there are not enough hours in the day to
work, eat, sleep and play,
Next I send my winter breezes accompanied by winter
sneezes,
I breathe on over-laden conker trees and then I see
chilly squirrels hurrying to and fro for hibernation,
Oh no here comes winter,
pushing me out the way with icy fingertips,
I'll be back next year . . .

Catherine Houlder (10)
St Patrick's Junior School, Woolston

ALL HALLOWS EVE

Pumpkins lit up in the windows
The haunting memories never go
Full moon in the sky
Deadly bats flying by
Zombies rising from the dead
Children laying scared in bed
Graveyard noises coming near,
People run scared in fear.

Nicholas Leon (11)
St Patrick's Junior School, Woolston

AUTUMN

On September 24th the wind blows,
the leaves rustle the colours of golden
brown and copper.

The sun goes down, the leaves fall,
the robins fly around all day long.

I walk through the dew in the morning and
I walk in the fields.

I see apples and blackberries. All the animals
are hibernating and it's time for me to . . .

Say goodbye!

Jessica Abbott (11)
St Patrick's Junior School, Woolston

LISTEN

Sshhh! Listen.
The waves crashing
Shells calling
Seagulls crowing
Crabs scuffling across the sand.
The chorus of the dolphins' cry
Roaming far and wide
Touching all in its path.
The breeze whistling in your ears
And the turtles burying their eggs
In the sand.

Listen . . . Listen . . .

Edward Goldring (10)
St Patrick's Junior School, Woolston

A Scary Night, An Awful Fright!

Witches on broomsticks,
Cackling by the stars,
As trick or treaters
Run past spraying paint onto cars.

Long, bony fingers tapping around you,
As ghosts and ghouls shout *boo!*

Zombies waking from their bed,
Into the graveyard land of the dead,
Bones snapping, knees cracking.

A scream quite far away,
The witches want to stay.

Kerry Colbert (10)
St Patrick's Junior School, Woolston

A Soggy Poem

Rain is gathering on the windowpane
Puddles are forming, rain is pouring
Walking down the road in saturated clothes
On the damp, soggy grass.
Clothes are sticking to me.
The weather is getting worse
All foggy and dull.

Gemma Champion (11)
St Patrick's Junior School, Woolston

Night Of The Broomsticks

Werewolves are howling.
Witches are cackling.

The stars twinkle in my face.
Witches having a broomstick race.

I'm standing in the corner,
Waiting for her.

The witch comes up to me.
I couldn't see her face.

Then I flew up into the air,
And I can see all the houses.

Children trick or treating,
And eating every sweet.

Vampires hiding behind walls.
Little children holding on to dolls.

Bats fly past the pale moon.
Hope I'm back home soon.

I am a witch's broomstick.

Natasha Nursing (11)
St Patrick's Junior School, Woolston

Drip, Drop

It's time to get up as the alarm clock rings,
Splashing water hitting the windowpanes.
I get out of bed to see rain pouring down,
And lots of puddles forming on the ground.

I walk down the stairs wondering what to do.
As I look out the window I feel I have the flu.
I step outside on the soaked and slippery doorstep,
Jumping through the puddles getting soaked to the skin.

Ashleen Stonadge (11)
St Patrick's Junior School, Woolston

LISTEN!

Listening, listening to the wind
high up in the sky
everything was quiet
but I don't know why.

All I could hear was some
shovelling sounds
and I think I can hear
the calling of hounds.

Listening, listening to the wind
high up in the sky
everything was quiet
but I don't know why.

The slight shudder of breeze
shuffled through my hair
I turned and looked back
but nothing was there.

Listening, listening to the wind
high up in the sky
everything was quiet
but I don't know why.

Thomas Draper (10)
St Patrick's Junior School, Woolston

TITANIC

A ship once sailed to America,
Titanic was its name,
They said it was unsinkable,
But it sank all the same.

It was her maiden voyage,
China finely polished,
They didn't realise that soon
The whole ship would be demolished.

She streamed through the water,
All hopes were set up high,
They didn't realise that soon,
All their dreams would die.

There was a great big scramble,
Who would get out first
Probably first class women and children,
The whole ship was cursed.

Death creeps up closer, too close,
Death sighs a mist across the water,
Its icy breath on your neck
It's you it's come to slaughter.

86 years have passed,
There's not much more to say,
Although it's still a tragedy,
To this very day.

Holly Colbert (10)
St Patrick's Junior School, Woolston

Autumn

Autumn days are getting colder
Autumn days are getting shorter
Autumn nights are getting longer
Autumn season is so fun because
Football season has just begun.

Rory McRae (11)
St Patrick's Junior School, Woolston

The Day The Aliens Attacked

'UFO' shouted Sam the sausage seller
Shrieks, shouts
Sirens sounded
On the day the aliens attacked

Screams, squabbling
Stillness hit Earth
On the day the aliens attacked

Tornadoes were launched, laser guns were brought
On the day the aliens attacked

The FBI and men in black were warned
The day the aliens attacked

Most people died, but some survived
On the day the aliens attacked

Some watched, some stared, some slept in bed, some swore
On the day the aliens attacked

They left the day after the attack
Thank goodness for that.

Nicholas Egleton (10)
Wimborne Junior School